MW01122012

2008 05 07

Margaret Atwood

A psychoanalytical study

Margaret Atwood
A psychoanalytical study

Rama Gupta

NEW DAWN PRESS, INC.
USA• UK• INDIA

NEW DAWN PRESS GROUP
Published by New Dawn Press Group
New Dawn Press, Inc., 244 South Randall Rd # 90, Elgin, IL 60123
e-mail: sales@newdawnpress.com

New Dawn Press, 2 Tintern Close, Slough, Berkshire, SL1-2TB, UK
e-mail: sterlingdis@yahoo.co.uk

New Dawn Press (An Imprint of Sterling Publishers (P) Ltd.)
A-59, Okhla Industrial Area, Phase-II, New Delhi-110020
e-mail: sterlingpublishers@airtelbroadband.in
www.sterlingpublishers.com

Margaret Atwood – A psychoanalytical study
© 2006, Rama Gupta
ISBN 1 932705 63 5

Courtesy: The cover photograph of Margaret Atwood is
by Mr S.K. Ghai

PRINTED IN INDIA

Preface

I wish to express my gratitude to Dr Usha Bande, Senior Lecturer, R.K.M.V., Shimla, under whose guidance this book was completed. It is a pleasure to acknowledge the debt I owe to Dr Usha Bande whose critical insight and precious counsel have benefited me immensely. But for her unfailing help and constant encouragement it would not have been possible for me to complete this book.

I record my warm thanks to Dr Bernard J. Paris, Professor, University of Florida (USA). Dr Usha Bande introduced me to his works on Karen Horney and their applicability to literature. I am grateful to him for sending me books which have been of immense help to me. I wonder if I could have completed this task without his timely help.

I express my gratitude to Shri Surinder Kumar Ghai for sending me material in shape of books, articles and research papers, which has been of great help to me. I would fail in my duty if I do not thank Mrs Geeta Ghai who has been very kind and hospitable during my stay with them. My deepest debts are due to my husband, Col. D. P. Gupta for providing me all comforts and time to accomplish the work. I record his constant help and guidance that made it possible for me to complete the book in time. Besides, in reading and re-reading the typed script, he took a keen interest and edited the typed pages meticulously.

I am also grateful to Miss Meenakshi, Librarian, Shastri Indo-Canadian Institute, New Delhi for allowing me to make use of the neatly arranged library and sending me material from Delhi and Canada.

I owe my gratitude to Shastri Indo-Canadian Institute; American Studies Research Centre, Hyderabad; American Centre, New Delhi; British Council Library, New Delhi and Himachal Pradesh University Library, Shimla.

I record my gratefulness to Principal Mrs Satish Verma, for her co-operation and encouragement.

I am grateful to Dr B. S. Pathania, Head of English Department and Dr Som P. Ranchan for their guidance and encouragement. They always displayed a keen interest in my work.

Shri P. C. Sharma who assisted in typesetting, deserves my special thanks for care and meticulousness with which he completed the work.

– Rama Gupta

Contents

Abbreviations Used

EW	The Edible Woman
S	Surfacing
LO	Lady Oracle
LBM	Life Before Man
BH	Bodily Harm
CE	Cat's Eye
NHG	Neurosis and Human Growth
MP	Motivation and Personality
TPB	Towards a Psychology of Being
OIC	Our Inner Conflicts

CHAPTER 1

Introduction

M argaret Atwood (b. 1939), poet, novelist, literary critic and
story writer, is a prominent figure in the contemporary
Canadian literature. She was born in Ottawa in Canada in 1939
and raised in Toronto. She graduated from the University of
Toronto in 1961 and did her Masters from Redcliff College,
Harvard University, in 1962. She came into limelight with the
Governor General's Award for her anthology of poems entitled
The Circle Game (1966). This was followed by the publication of
Survival (1972) which brought her further acclaim. The same year,
Surfacing, with its feminist and nationalist slant, established her
reputation internationally. Since the appearance of her first book
of poems, *Double Persephone* (1961), Atwood has published several
other volumes of poetry and won many awards. In 1977 she
received the City of Toronto Book Award as well as The Canadian
Booksellers' Association Award for *Lady Oracle*. Her other novel
Alias Grace won the Giller Prize in Canada and Premio Mondello
in Italy; and her most recent *The Blind Assassin* is the winner of the
2002 Booker Prize. Atwood has taught at several Canadian
universities and also worked as an editor with the House of
Anansi Press. She was a spokesperson for Amnesty International
and President of Pen International.

The fact that Margaret Atwood, a versatile Canadian writer of
today, did not want to be recognised as a Canadian writer in 1960
is not at all surprising when we take into account the fact that the
Canadian fiction of the early decades of the nineteenth century
was not much popular. According to Frye, it was formula writing.
Margaret Atwood herself reiterated this fact in "Surviving the
Eighties" when she said, "Although we wanted to become writers,
we certainly didn't want to become Canadian writers..." A
Canadian writer for her was an "oxymoron". According to her,

"one could hardly expect us to make a living at it, and anything resembling the American notion of literary success was out of the question. Canadian books were routinely not taught in schools and universities. I myself have never taken a course on Canadian literature".[1] Like other writers of her time, she also read Sartre and Beckett. "Literature" meant British literature with "Shakespeare, Eliot, Austen, Thomas Hardy, Keats and Wordsworth and Shelley and Byron" (p. 232). It was at Harvard that Atwood first began to think seriously about Canada. Therefore, she was not only influenced by Northrop Frye and Harward's Perry Miller but also by her predecessors like A. J. M. Smith, Dorothy Livesay and Al Purdy. The poetry of Pratt, Jay MacPherson, Margaret Avison, P. K. Page and Davidson attracted her and moulded her literary career. According to Davidsons:

> *The new feminism, a myth-centred poetry, Frye's criticism and the growing nationalism of the early sixties all helped to shape Atwood's literary inheritance: together they produced a particular sensibility, a mythic imagination reflected in her treatment of the male-female relationship and Canadian nature.*[2]

As regards the Canadian fiction that was written before 1900, only a few books deserve mention: Susanna Moodie's *Roughing it in the Bush* and Major John Richardson's novel *Wacousta* (1832). F. P. Grove and Grey Own, two prominent Canadian writers, set the trend of taking on fabricated identities. Apart from Kreotsch's novels *The Studhorse Man* and *Gone Indian*, characters in other novels such as Margaret Laurence's *The Fire Dwellers*, Robertson Davies's *The World of Wonders* and Margaret Atwood's *Lady Oracle* took on fabricated identities.

Atwood's fiction cannot be fixed within the conventional labels like feminist, nationalist, modernist and post-modernist. It is not because she herself disclaims these labels but because of the fact that she is a diverse and elusive writer. Sherill Grace observes that "such a versatile and evolving writer" cannot be fixed in a phrase. Atwood's concern goes much beyond. She calls for the creation and acceptance of female characters who are fully human with all their individuality and variety. However, she has been instrumental in shaping Canada's understanding of herself. Her *Survival* played a significant role in this regard. *Survival* located the Canadian "here" by providing a map so that they could see themselves in relation to everything else. She contends that "Canada is an unknown territory for the people who lives in it"[3]. It provided a national myth and it could compete with the American Frontier myth. *Survival* established the fact that there was a Canadian literature. It is in this that *Survival's* importance lies; it created a sense of "being" that Canadians are; Canadian literature is. It was not merely a major publishing success but as Rosenberg says, "the most visible, widely read critical work on Canadian literature in Canada's history".[4] Atwood herself admits that she became "a thing... a culmination of being an icon, that is something that people worship, and being a target, that is something they shoot at "(qtd. in Rosenberg 134). To Atwood it is "a personal statement" and "political manifesto" (*Survival*, p. 13) but critics judged it as centralist, historic and non-evaluative. However, the book's literary if not critical, achievement is undeniable. J. Lee Thomson does not consider it whimsical to think if Canada and Canadian Literature could have survived "without, in one form or another, *Survival*."[5] Even to George Woodcock, *Survival* is "interesting and exciting as an index to the development of our (Canadian) Literary tradition."[6] According to B. W. Powe, Canadians felt "insecure and isolated particularly because of their proximity to the American literary machine and so felt the need to express a difference."[7] *Survival* expresses just that: "a difference."

Margaret Atwood's characters are motivated by intra-psychic and interpersonal conflicts. Her protagonists are obsessed with some kind of fear which leads them either to hide their identity or to assume double identity so as to escape reality. All of them are self-alienated. It is felt that the motivational system of these characters can be understood if we study them in the light of Horneyan tenets. After all, these characters are human beings placed in different situations. They move in their particular social and cultural settings and react to them in peculiar manners according to their motivation systems. Karen Horney's theory presents us with suitable tools to understand these characters.

Third Force Psychology

In literary criticism, the term "Third Force Psychology"[8] came into focus in 1964 when B. J. Paris, an exponent in the field, started analysing literary characters with the help of the psychological theories of Karen Horney and Abraham Maslow. In the field of psychology, however, the term was in vogue since 1962. It was Abraham Maslow who used it for the first time in the preface to *Towards a Psychology of Being* for all those psychologists who gave a comprehensive view of human nature distinct from that of the Freudians and the behaviourists. It follows then, that Third Force Psychology is not a new branch of psychology. It includes what Maslow termed the "splinter groups", who coalesced and formed a "Third Force". These are: Adler and his followers, Jungians, Neo-Freudians, Post-Freudians, Otto Rank and his followers, Gestalt therapists, Self-psychologists, phenomenological psychologists, humanitarian psychologists, Rogerians and growth-psychologists. Since all these theorists offered a holistic and optimistic view of human nature, they came to be known as "humanistic psychologists".

According to Third Force psychologists, man is not a tension-reducing machine, nor is he a conditional animal; man has in him a third force, an "evolutionary constructive" force which inspires him to strive for self-realisation. Man has the intrinsic potential to reach the goal of self-fulfilment but unfortunately, his efforts are forestalled in life by unhealthy or injurious influences. All Third Force psychologists see self-realisation as the highest value for a human being. It means that he has the potential to be "fully human". Different psychologists give it different names: self-actualisation, individuation, autonomy, integration, self-realisation. Whatever be the name, the goal is the same: realisation of the highest potential.

The field of Third Force is vast and the psychologists comprising this branch are numerous. However, I shall only expound the theory of Karen Horney and refer to Abraham Maslow and Erich Fromm as and when necessary. I have delimited my field in order to achieve sharper focus so as to be precise in my analysis.

Karen Horney, like other Third Force psychologists, insists on the need to realise the real self. Real self for her is the foundation of personality. It is the central inner force which is common to all human beings but it is unique in each. As she observes, these are "The unique alive forces of his real self: the clarity and depth of his feelings, thoughts, wishes, interests; the ability to tap his own resources, the strength of his willpower; the special capacities or gifts he may have; the faculty to express himself to others with his spontaneous feelings. All this will in time enable him to find his set of values and his aims in life."[9] Horney has "the belief in the inherent urge to grow." For her, the real self is "the original" force that leads towards individual growth. It is this real self we are looking for "when we say that we want to find ourselves" (NHG, p. 158). Given a favourable environment, warmth of affection, inner security and inner freedom, the child learns to live according to his real self.

As Horney sees it, an unfavourable or adverse condition in his environment produces in a child a feeling of "basic anxiety". Horney describes basic anxiety as the "feeling of being isolated and helpless in a world conceived as potentially hostile" (NHG, p. 18). These feelings arise in childhood when one does not get favourable conditions to grow according to his individual needs. Children whose parents don't give them genuine love, lose the sense of belonging, the "we" feeling. They develop "profound insecurity and vague apprehensions" (NHG, p. 18).

A child's urge for safety, warmth and love are so strong that when he fails to get these, he abandons his real self. As Maslow puts it, "The primary choice is between others and one's own self. If the only way to maintain the self is to lose the other, than the ordinary child will give up the self."[10] Erich Fromm also recognises the importance of relatedness. He describes the emergence of individuation as the process of "growing aloneness". When it happens, a child may submerge himself in the outside world or give in to hostile feelings. Or he may develop in a productive way. He may establish a spontaneous relationship with man and nature. According to Erich Fromm, if every step in the direction of separation and individuation were matched by "corresponding growth of the self, the development of the child would be harmonious."[11] He also points out that while the individuation is an automatic process, growth of the self is affected by various social and personal factors.

In *The Neurotic Personality of Our Time*[12] (1987), Karen Horney makes it clear that childhood experiences determine conditions for neurosis but they cannot be considered the only cause of later troubles. Like other Third Force psychologists, she does not deny the role of childhood environment in shaping the neurotic drives of an individual but stresses on the present structure of the psyche and refutes the Freudian theory that adult reactions are the repetition of infantile experiences. She emphasises that once the child starts feeling "basic anxiety," he resorts to certain defensive strategies to deal with the conditions arising out of his fears and inadequacy. Later his particular system develops under the influence of external factors such as familial atmosphere, social and cultural exigencies. His internal necessities to feel whole, and external pressures, mould his adult character.

Horney, Maslow and Fromm are of the view that specific social and cultural conditions generate neurotic trends. Maslow terms neurosis, a deficiency disease and Horney classifies it as a deviation from the normal pattern of social behaviour. "Most neurosis involved, along with other complex determinants, ungratified wishes for safety, for belongingness and identifications for close relationships and for respect and prestige" (TPB, p. 21). Social-psychologists emphasise the role of social and cultural forces in shaping man's responses to his surroundings. Erich Fromm affirms that even the most beautiful and the most ugly inclination of man are not a part of his biological fixed nature, "but result from the social process which creates man."[13] Man's self-consciousness helps him to think of himself as a whole. His interactions with other members of the society enable him to bring himself within his own experimental purview. "Thus he can consciously integrate and unify the various aspects of his self, to form a single consistent and coherent and organized personality."[14]

According to Horney, when a child sees a "potentially hostile" environment, he feels threatened and does not relate himself to others with his real self but with his compulsive drives. "He cannot simply like or dislike, trust or distrust, express his wishes or protest against those of others but has automatically to devise ways to cope with people and to manipulate them with minimum damage to himself."[15] This process weakens the real self and he reacts to his environment with fears. It produces in him a dread of himself and others. He feels angry and hostile but helpless to express his danger in this threatening environment. When he represses his hostility, he feels unworthy, unlovable, weak and impotent. To compensate for his feelings of worthlessness and inadequacy, he lifts himself above others by seeking self-glorification. This he does by adopting interpersonal strategies of defence.

These three solutions are: his move towards people, move away from people and move against people. The selection of these strategies of defence depends upon his individual temperament, his social or familial conditions. A person is driven by the compulsive nature of his inner necessities. A child who moves towards people adopts compliant or self-effacing characteristics. In his move against people, he adopts an aggressive trend. Those who move away from people become detached. The above three solutions are not mutually exclusive strategies. The individual may move from one solution to another to gain some sense of wholeness and ability to function but he will not be able to resolve his basic conflict.

The three interpersonal moves give us a picture of character "types" but in life, "people tending towards the same main solution" may differ in their human qualities, gifts or achievements. As Horney puts it:

> *Moreover, what we regard as "types" are actually cross sections of personalities in which the neurotic process had led to rather extreme developments with pronounced characteristics. But there is always an indeterminate range of intermediate structure deriding any precise qualifications. These complexities are further enhanced by the fact that, owing to the process of psychic fragmentation, even in extreme instances, there is often more than one main solution. "Most cases are mixed cases" says William James, "and we should not treat our classification with too much respect." Perhaps it would be more correct to speak of directions of development than of types (NHG, p. 191).*

Under the compliant solution, Horney lists two types; (i) self-effacing and (ii) morbidly dependent. For both types, "salvation lies in others" (NHG, p. 226). The self-effacing person in his move to others, "tends to subordinate himself, takes second place, leaving the limelight to others" (OIC, p. 52). He shuns "everything that is presumptuous, selfish and aggressive." He cultivates all qualities of helplessness and martyrdom and expects protection and love in return. He values attributes of goodness and usefulness. His bargain is that if he is good, loving and noble, he will be treated well by fate and other people. But when he is not valued for the "lovable" qualities and his virtues are not rewarded, he retaliates. Since he is a self-effacing person, he cannot be violent. Therefore, he turns his anger inward and feels weak to fight in self-interest. This initiates his "shrinking process." So he despairs divine justice, indulges in self-pity, guilty feelings and personal inadequacy. When he cannot live up to the dictates of his solution, his inner rage threatens his self-image. Self-hate is generated. His 'shoulds' and neurotic claims give rise to tensions. He is torn by inner conflicts. It results, in extreme cases, in vindictiveness. It may take any form depending upon individual temperament and how much he is damaged.

Erotic love fascinates a morbidly dependent individual. For him, love is "the ticket to paradise, where all woes end: no more feeling lost, guilty, and unworthy; no more responsibility for self; no more struggle with a harsh world for which he feels helplessly unequipped" (NHG, p. 239). He is attracted to a masterful, expansive and proud person. This not only meets his need for surrender and safe expression of his aggressive tendencies but he also derives vicarious strength. Being an epitome of all lovable qualities, he feels hurt and disillusioned if his qualities are not recognised. It means total rejection of himself and like the self-effacing type, he also reacts in a self-destructive way.

In order to master life and to become successful, an aggressive type makes a move against people and cultivates efficiency and resourcefulness. He becomes aggressive and self-aggrandised. There are three sub-types of this expansive solution: the narcissistic; the perfectionists; and the arrogant-vindictive. They all "aim at mastering life. This is their way of conquering fears and anxieties; this gives meaning to their lives and gives them a certain zest for living" (NHG, p. 212). The narcissist seeks to master life by self-admiration and the exercise of charm. He believes he is the "anointed, the man of destiny, the prophet, the great giver, the benefactor of mankind" (NHG, p. 194). The perfectionist chases standards of perfection and excellence. His own perfection therefore is "not only a means to superiority but also one to control life" (NHG, p. 197). An arrogant-vindictive person has a compulsive need for vindictive triumph. These aggressive types are proud of their self-sufficiency. They deny all softer feelings, compassion, consideration, loyalty and self-sacrifice. They do not depend on the world to reward them. They seek "callous pursuit of self-interest" and that is "the paramount law" (OIC, p. 64) for them. They are too certain of achieving their aspirations if they remain true to their vision of life.

The basically detached person seeks neither love nor mastery. He wants to be left alone. He expects nothing and wants to have nothing expected of him. His bargain is that if he asks nothing, they will not bother him, that if he tries for nothing, he will not fail and that if he expects little of life, he will not be disappointed. He feels superior to others in his independence. But his freedom is meaningless because he is alienated from his spontaneous desires. This involves not only living in the imagination but shrinking his inner cravings. In order to resolve his basic conflict he draws a magic circle so that no one can penetrate. He resorts to "escape and hide". His resignation from active living gives him an "onlooker" attitude but this is "no true solution because the compulsive cravings for closeness as well as for aggressive domination, exploitation, and excelling remain, and they keep harassing if not paralyzing their carrier" (OIC, p. 95). Thus, he develops a contradictory set of values and this is self-destructive. This intensifies his original feelings of worthlessness and self-alienation and creates a basic inner conflict which takes him away from his real self.

Horney stresses that when interpersonal strategies work to defend against basic anxiety, the intra-psychic forces are also active, and they create problems for him. When he is gripped by self-hate and is weak because of self-alienation, he creates an idealised image of himself. He endows himself with "unlimited powers and with exalted faculties; he becomes a hero, a genius, a supreme lover, a saint, a god" (NHG, p. 22). In this, he poses superior, and is elevated in his sense of significance. His picture of himself depends upon his strategy. For an aggressive individual, his heroism, leadership or strength gives him an identity. Thus harbouring his imaginary pictures, he strives to live up to them. He directs all his efforts towards actualising a false image and forsaking the real self. The creation of the idealised image produces not only the search for glory but a whole structure of neurotic strategies. These strategies are self-glorification, neurotic claims, tyrannical shoulds and neurotic pride. Horney calls this structure of intra-psychic defence, "the pride system."

In his search for glory, the individual feels "he is entitled to be treated by others, or by fate, in accord with his grandiose notions about himself" (NHG, p. 41). He not only nourishes grandiose notions about himself but makes neurotic claims on others too. As Horney says, the function of neurotic claims is to perpetuate the individual's "illusions about himself, and to shift responsibility to factors outside himself" (NHG, p. 63). Though these are illusions he is harbouring about himself, he is unaware of it. The result is that they increase his vulnerability and "prevent him from squaring himself with his difficulties" (NHG, p. 63). They perpetuate rather than alleviate the individual's difficulties. Side by side his shoulds make a claim on him. He "should" be as he visualises himself to be. These inner dictates set standards for him. All his energies, which should take a normal person towards self-actualisation, drag him to actualise the idealised self.

The "shoulds" and the neurotic claims are very damaging. They shatter in the face of the realities of life. When they are shattered, the neurotic pride suffers a blow and tension mounts. In order to restore his pride, the neurotic takes recourse to various methods, depending upon his temperament. Sometimes he hits harder or sometimes he tries to forget the incident. It is clear that both ways his idealised self creates an impossible situation for him. To live up to his glorified image, he makes tremendous efforts but when he fails he feels the onslaught of self-hate.

Healthy pride is important for the self but neurotic pride is "the climax and consolidation of the process initiated with the search of glory" (NHG, p. 109). It is not only based on illusions and self-deception but also on his imagined attributes. This pride system is, in fact, his defence against self-hate. Threats to it produce anxiety and hostility. Its collapse results in self-hate. Feelings of shame and humiliation overpower him. He indulges in self-hate. Self-hate is essentially the rage that the idealised self feels towards the actual self for not being what it should. Horney contends that the neurotic has to counter four selves; the real self which is already banished; the idealised self which is impossible to attain, the despised self and the actual self that he is, at a given moment. According to Horney, when the real self is forsaken, alienation takes hold of a person. Self-hate and inner conflict produce a rift in the personality and an inner war starts. Unable to bear the onslaught of self-condemnation, self-accusation and self-hate, he snaps his bonds with reality. There is no spontaneous integration. He cannot lead a goal-directed life and fights a desperate battle against the world. He goes to hell within himself and it leads to tragic results. Karen Horney views neurotic development as a process of becoming alienated from the real self. What Horney terms the real self, Matthew Arnold calls it the "best self" which culture nourishes. It unites us in harmony with ourselves. "This is the very self which culture, or the study of perfection, seeks to develop in us; at the expense of our old untransformed self, taking pleasure only in doing what it likes or is used to do and exposing us to the risk of clashing with everyone who is doing the same."[16] It is, therefore, essential to seek our best self and affirm it with all our strength.

Karen Horney's theory has provided us a tool for psychoanalytic study of characters. Paris affirms that "Third Force" is a powerful tool of critical, biographical and cultural analysis. In literary criticism, these theories can be employed in three ways: "to analyze literary characters in motivational terms; to analyze the implied authors of individual works, showing their inner conflicts and blind spots; and to analyze the possibility of the author as it can be inferred from all his work."[17] When psychology is used to interpret literature, critics often question the viability of this approach. They contend that by bringing in extra-literary material to understand literature we are failing to read a novel as a novel. Psychological critics on the other hand assert that in a psychological approach we may bring material outside of literary studies, but we use it within the framework of a literary form. According to a critic, by using the tool of psychology, we enlarge and deepen our conception of human nature by understanding human emotions and motivations. We cannot understand, a critic says, "the meaning of literary works without an extensive knowledge of human emotions and motivations."[18] A realistic novel creates a fictional world of its own with the help of representation and interpretation. While the former governs the rhetoric, the latter deals with the mimesis of the work. To comprehend a character, his motives and actions, a critic must recognise the disparity between representation and interpretation, rhetoric and mimesis. Horneyan tenets can illuminate us by enabling us to recognise the inconsistencies without rationalisation or reduction.

Margaret Atwood's characters have often been called neurotics, but it would be unjust to dump them all under one category. They are after all human beings. Some of them are accomplished artists whose needs and demands should be admitted. In the following chapters in which I will be discussing six novels of Atwood, namely: *The Edible Woman, Surfacing, Lady Oracle, Life before Man, Bodily Harm and Cat's Eye,* I shall endeavour to understand the intra-psychic and interpersonal problems of the characters and to see them as human beings.

References

1. Margaret Atwood, "Canadian-American Relations: Surviving The Eighties," *Glimpses of Canadian Literature* ed., C. D. Narasimhaiah and C. N. Srinath Wendy Keitner (Mysore: Dhvanyaloka Publication, 1985), pp. 235-36.

2. Arnold E. and Cathy N. Davidson, *The Art of Margaret Atwood: Essays in Criticism* (Anansi: Toronto, 1981), p. 21.

3. Margaret Atwood, *Survival: A Thematic Guide to Canadian Literature* (Toronto: Anansi, 1972), p. 18.

4. Jerome H. Rosenberg, *Margaret Atwood* (Boston: Twayne Publishers, 1984), p. 135.

5. J. Lee Thomson, "Can Canada Survive *Survival?* An Article on Survival: A Thematic Guide to Canadian Literature," *American Review of Canadian Studies* 3.2 (Autumn 1973), pp. 101-7.

6. George Woodcock, *The World of Canadian Writing: Critiques & Recollections* (Vancouver: University of Washington Press, 1980), p. 160.

7. B. W. Powe, *A Climate Changed: Essays on Canadian Writers* (Oakville, Ont: Mosaic Press, 1984), p. 73.

8. Bernard J. Paris, "Horney, Maslow and Third Force," in B. J. Paris, ed. *Third Force Psychology and the Study of Literature* (Toronto: Associated University Press, 1986).

9. Karen Horney, *Neurosis and Human Growth* (New York: W. W. Norton & Company, 1950), p. 17. Further references are from this edition and will be cited as NHG along with pagination.

10. Abraham Maslow, *Toward a Psychology of Being*, 2nd ed. (New York: D. Van Nostrand, 1968), p. 50. Further references are from this edition and will be cited as TPB along with pagination.

11. Erich Fromm, *The Fear of Freedom* (1942; rpt. London: Routledge and Kagan Paul, 1960), p. 25.

12. Karen Horney, *The Neurotic Personality of Our Time* (New York: Norton, 1937).

13. Erich Fromm, *Escape From Freedom* (1941; rpt. New York: Hall, Rinehart and Winson, 1964), p. 12.

14. George Herbert Mead, *On Social Psychology*, ed. Anselm Strauss (1956; rpt. Chicago: University of Chicago Press, 1964), p. 269.

15. Karen Horney, *Our Inner Conflicts* (New York: Norton, 1945), p. 219. Referred to as OIC.

16. Matthew Arnold, *Culture and Anarchy*, ed. J. Dover Wilson (Cambridge: University Press, 1971), p. 95.

17. Bernard J. Paris, *Third Force Psychology and the Study of Literature*, p. 61.

18. Norman Friedman, "Psychology and Literary Form: Toward a Unified Approach," in *Third Force Psychology and the Study of Literature*, op. cit., p. 98.

CHAPTER 2

The Edible Woman

Margaret Atwood's first novel, *The Edible Woman* deals with Marian MacAlpin's predicament. Marian MacAlpin, the protagonist of this novel, is a young graduate who works for Seymour Surveys for consumer products. She is engaged to a handsome, upcoming young lawyer, Peter, whose hobbies are collection of guns and cameras. At some point after their relationship, Marian loses hold on herself and becomes obsessed with the fear that she is just an object or a consumable item. Threatened with this fear, Marian runs from one relationship to another but these escapes do not quell her fears. Towards the end of the novel, she bakes a large cake in the shape of a woman and offers it as a woman's substitute to Peter thus symbolically refusing to be a victim. This symbolic act relieves her of her irrational fear.

Marian's condition has been variously explored by critics. Wayne Fraser sees it as "the difficulties for the women of the 1960s, of living within conventional norms." He views this as "the growing threat to a woman's identity by a male-controlled and increasingly consumer-oriented society."[1] Annette Kolodny finds it impossible to live "authentically amid the self-induced delusions of consumer society."[2] Others relate it to the central fact of victimisation and explore this victim position as "occupied by women in a patriarchal, capitalistic, consumer society."[3] To Gayle Green, Marian's position reflects the "similarity between woman's position in the alienated world of work and her sexual objectification,"[4] as representative of female experience in Canada. To Elizabeth Brady, Atwood's real achievement in *The Edible Woman*, is to have examined the "inter-relationships between the various forms which male domination assumes in a woman's life, and then to have related these forms to the larger domination structure of consumer capitalism."[5]

The consumer world in which Marian inhabits, appropriates Marian's identity and reduces her to an "in between thing or mindless body". But there is something more to it. Marian's problem is one of 'becoming', which according to Erich Fromm is both a metaphysical and socio-political problem. "I couldn't become one of the men upstairs; I couldn't become a machine person or one of the questionnaire-marking ladies, as that would be a step down" (EW, p. 20). At the metaphysical plane, Marian's quest is for a meaningful human identity; at the socio-political level, her quest is to become neither a man nor a machine but a woman with an absolute, as against a relatively defined, identity. In fact, Marian's mental, moral and emotional issues oscillate between two polarities of "yes" and "no" to the involvement with Peter. But her final resolution to say "no" to her meaningless existence is achieved after a prolonged period of intra-psychic and interpersonal conflicts. She shifts from compliance to rebellion, back and forth. Since she vacillates between changing strategies, her behaviour is inconsistent and leaves much scope for disparity between thinking and action. She lives in fear and grows increasingly alienated from the society. She has a problem in establishing a working relationship with the "real" world. Hence, it can be better understood in the context of Karen Horney's tenets of psychology.

To understand the psychological complexities of her adult character, we may as well consider her childhood since the narrator gives us sufficient clues to her childhood. We know that Marian was expected to measure up to the expectations of her parents. Marian takes a secret pleasure in the thought that her expected marriage will please her parents because this was what "they've been waiting for" (EW, p. 103). Her thoughts, turning again and again to the approval of her parents, are not meaningless. They show her deep-rooted desire to measure up to the expectations of her parents and aunts. A similar situation is depicted in Anita Desai's *Bye-Bye Blackbird*.[6] Sarah marries an Indian much against the wishes of her parents. But, parental approval/disapproval, though disregarded initially in the heat of the first flush of love, suddenly acquires gigantic dimensions and Sarah feels miserable for having disregarded her parents' wishes.

In Marian's case, she has not taken any step against her parents' wishes, but she knows that her decisions would affect them. She has "led a sheltered life," and she conforms to this accepted social role of a "good" girl.

Her parents' "fears" about the effects of her university education are calmed but her process of alienation starts from this point. She is doing what she should, not what she desires. Raised in a stereotyped family, her attitude towards traditionally learnt sex roles is understandable. That is why she views a single parenthood of Ainsley with disapproving eyes. She is intolerant of any reversal of these parenting roles. She thinks of marriage and children in terms of legitimate or illegitimate. Ainsley calls her 'prude' when she discovers that Marian holds either/or attitude to career and marriage. Her familial atmosphere is not congenial for her healthy development. She does not talk of the love of her parents. She does not wish to visit them unless she has to say something which would please them. This type of atmosphere leads to lack of personal involvement. Marian also lacks a sense of belonging. "Belonging... means a subjective feeling of one's personal involvement to the extent that one feels himself to be an integral and indispensable part of the system."[7] She has neither love nor sharing of life with family, hence, she becomes more alienated. Erich Fromm maintains that by uniting himself with other persons in the spirit of love and shared work, he can hope to end his alienation.

A way out of this is the adoption of some psychological prop. Marian desperately needs someone to belong to. Although she has made a workable "arrangement" with Ainsley, it is limited only to the sharing of an apartment. It does not give her a sense of security and belongingness. Peter is the first and the only person to take her out of this growing alienation and insecurity. When we seriously enquire into the imperative of her basic need, we understand why her attitude becomes one of self-effacement. She herself admits that "I was being self-effacing on purpose" (EW, p. 71). Being a self-effacing person, Marian's wish is never to displease Peter. Since pleasing Peter is of great importance to her, it becomes her primary concern and subsequently her anxiety. In order to remain his adored self, she leans more and more on him. She is dedicated to Peter and does not want to assert her independent will. She sees him as "a rescuer from chaos, a provider of stability" (EW, p. 89).

Marrying Peter means having someone who would take over her life and would make decisions for her. It is clear when she coyly tells Peter that she would rather leave big decisions up to him and adds "The funny thing was I really meant it" (EW, p. 90). But this decision of marrying Peter is need-based and shows her basic anxiety. Seen from the perspective of her psychological compulsion, it is understandable why she has become passive and powerless. She is happy:

> *That it was my aura of independence and common sense he had liked; he saw me as the kind of girl who wouldn't try to take over his life. He had recently had an unpleasant experience with what he called "the other kind." That was the assumption we had been working on, and it has suited me. We had been taking each other at our face values, which meant we had got on very well. Of course I had to adjust to his moods, but that's true of any man and his were too obvious to cause much difficulty (EW, p. 61).*

She is ready to take on the role of the subservient wife. Feminist scholars are rather critical of this attitude. Shannon feels that Marian, the "central female character remains confused in her identity and muted in her speech because she is defined in relation to "Americanized" males."[8] According to Salat, Peter, Marian's Fiancé "with his unqualified desire to dominate and colonize Marian, emblematizes the archetypical male principle."[9] Marian herself fears this domination and his wish to possess her completely. She remarks "now that she had been ringed, he took pride in displaying her" (EW, p. 176). When seen from the Horneyan angle, we understand the reason behind Peter's wish to colonise and Marian's fear of domination.

To surrender to a stronger personality is inherent in a dependant character. Marian is a compliant character and allows this deal to materialise. She poses to be good without pride and hopes she will be treated well by Peter. The complicity, in the case of Marian, is self-inflicted, reprehensible and undesirable. Linda Hutcheon remarks: "As both a Canadian and a woman, she protests any tendency towards passivity and naivety; she refuses to allow either Canadian or women to deny their complicity in the power structure that may subject them."[10] It is not a healthy drive but a compulsive one; subservience is the need of the self-effacing character. This can be seen in Horneyan terms as her urgent need to lift herself above others. Discussing the need for self-glorification, Horney contends that if a person has "a sense of belonging, his feeling inferior to others would not be so serious a handicap. But living in a competitive society, and feeling at bottom—as he does—isolated and hostile, he can only develop an urgent need to lift himself above others" (NHG, p. 21). Keeping in mind Marian's panic at the prospect of becoming a spinster pensioner of Seymour Surveys, we understand that she has already subconsciously accepted this subservient wifely role as her ultimate destiny.

She looks up to Peter as her ideal choice. "He's attractive and he's bound to be successful, and also he's neat, which is a major point when you're going to be living with someone" (EW, p. 102). Marian admires him for his superiority and believes in his intellect. Through him she obtains the supreme confirmation of herself. She derives vicarious power from Peter. Her relation with him permits her to satisfy her self-effacing and her expansive drives. When she gives over the direction of her life to him, she satisfies her need for fusion and dependency. Her ability to attract a person like Peter gives her a sense of great power as well as "triumphant elation" that Peter honours her qualities. Peter says, "I don't know what I'd do if you didn't understand. Most women wouldn't, but you're so sensible" (EW, p. 64). She enjoys "The sense of proud ownership she felt at being with him there in that more or less public way caused her to reach across the table and take his hand" (EW, pp. 146-47). Alan Howe calls *The Edible Woman* "a novel about choices" but Marian, cannot choose. She cannot choose either to be a "scheming super female" like Ainsley or the earthmother like Clara. She cannot be like "office virgins" because this opportunism is self-destructive for her. In Marian's rejection of these choices, a scholar sees Atwood's attitude: "Atwood is neither a hard-core feminist nor an anti-feminist but a clear-sighted humanist."[11] In fact, for a compliant character like Marian there is no choice but a compulsive drive to be good and self-sacrificing. Her identity and choice lie in keeping intact her idealised wifely image.

Marian establishes her uniqueness and self-importance by complimenting herself on her moral superiority to Ainsley and Clara. She maintains her separate identity by feeling superior to "immoral" Ainsley. "I've never been silly about marriage the way Ainsley is. She's against it on principle, and life isn't run by principles but by adjustment" (EW, p. 102). She justifies her decision of marrying Peter, "it is actually a very good step to take. Of course, I'd always assumed through high school and college that I was going to marry someone eventually and have children, everyone does" (EW, pp. 101-102). She is glad she "wasn't Clara" who "lets herself be treated like a thing!" (EW, p. 38). These assessments help her raise her self-esteem and realise her idealised image.

In this initial phase of relationship with Peter, she comes closer than she ever had to feeling that she is her idealised self. Marian's loss of individuality is indicated by the silencing of her inner voice of ironic commentary. She begins to quote Peter to herself in private as an infallible authority and thus becomes "Her Master's Voice." As Peter says: "You can't continue to run around indefinitely." Peter says: People who are not married "get funny in middle age," according to him, they get "embittered or addled or something" (EW, p. 102). Thus, she gloats over his authority and sees herself as "small and oval, mirrored in his eyes" (EW, p. 83). This image conveys that henceforth she will strive to be the mirror reflection of the ideal that Peter imagines her to be.

As long as Peter honours the claims of her bargain, Marian remains "marvellous Marian." Peter's treatment in Plaza restaurant deals Marian's image a devastating blow. She feels hurt, rejected and neglected when Peter shows attention to Len and Ainsley. She feels 'deflated', her pride is crushed. She cannot afford his condemnation which is evident in his remarks: "Didn't think your were the hysterical type" (EW, p. 74) as her self-esteem is all dependent on his approval. She has glorified Peter, transferred her pride to him, made him the measure of her worth. Describing the importance of love for a self-effacing person, Horney emphatically maintains that this type cannot stand being alone and ignored. As a result she has very little defence-mechanism against his adverse judgement. She indulges in "passive externalization" which according to Horney, "shows in her being accused by others, suspected or neglected, kept down, treated with contempt, abused, exploited or treated with outright cruelty" (NHG, p. 255). When slighted, Marian suddenly becomes aggressive and accuses Peter of "being plain ordinary rude!" (EW, p. 80). She is overcome by rage, she feels the fury of rejection.

Now we are in a position to understand Marian's behaviour during her crisis: her sudden flight after drinks at Park Plaza and her hiding under Len's bed. They are her defence strategies to restore her dwindling sense of significance and to save her from self-hate. She has outwardly accepted the pattern of passive femininity expected by Peter but inwardly she is withdrawing from this version of womanhood. It is evident in the contention of Peter, "The trouble with you," is "you're just rejecting your femininity" (EW, p. 80). It would, however, be more appropriate to infer that she is desperately struggling to restore her pride first by refusing to accept that Peter is neglecting her, and then by exonerating him of all blame. "He was treating me a stage-prop; silent but solid, a two-dimensional outline. He wasn't ignoring me, as perhaps I had felt – he was depending on me" (EW, p. 71). When this posture fails to uplift her, she gains vindictive triumph by running along Plaza streets. She herself confesses, "it seemed an achievement, and accomplishment of some kind to put them one by one behind me" (EW, p. 72). She feels happy that Peter and his friends had to chase her. Christine Gomez sees in Marian's refusal to accept her victim situation a clear case of her victimisation. That Atwood is sensitive about victimisation is evident in *Survival* [12] where she deals with four stages in the victimisation process. This shall be discussed at length in the next chapter.

Marian suffers an identity crisis when she wrestles with her growing awareness of her dual, if not multiple, personalities which surface after she has rejected her imposed image. The conflict between her compliant and aggressive trends produces much of Marian's emotional and intellectual turmoil and drives her into inconsistent behaviour. Sometimes she runs away from Peter while at others she wants to be forgiven. "I was filled with penitence, but there was no outlet for it. If I could be alone with Peter it would be different, I thought: he could forgive me" (EW, p. 75). Then she goes to Duncan in order to feel triumphant and shows flagrant disregard for her involvement with Peter. She baffles Peter by her behaviour. She herself is aware of this inconsistency. "The way I went about doing things may have been a little inconsistent with my true personality" (EW, p. 101). But she cannot help it. Her inability to arrive at a decision is expressed in the following remarks:

> *However, it had left me in a sort of vacuum. Peter and I had avoided talking about the future because we knew it didn't matter: We weren't really involved. Now, though, something in me had decided we were involved: surely that was the explanation for the powder-room collapse and the flight. I was evading reality. Now, this very moment, I would have to face it. I would have to decide what I wanted to do (EW, p. 77).*

The conflict between her expansive and compliant drives drags Peter and Marian apart making it difficult for each to comprehend the motive of the other. Peter has his own compulsions to deal with. He wants to marry Marian out of his need of profession where a single person is not taken seriously. Reflecting on his marriage he says, "It'll be a lot better in the long run for my practice too, the clients like to know you've got a wife; people get suspicious of a single man after a certain age, they start thinking you're a queer or something" (EW, p. 89). He finds his job profitable and his common routine activities more fascinating and fulfilling. He is an expansive person who wants mastery over life. Individuals like him resent those who depend too much on them because, conversely, they are scared that such a person may take over their life.

For Peter, Marian is a girl he can always depend on. The kind of girl who "wouldn't try to take over his life" (EW, p. 61). Peter shifts his energies towards his business so as to escape intra-psychic and interpersonal conflicts. He is a perfectionist who has ordered his thoughts, life, learning and career into a near-perfect pattern. He could be described as "ordinariness raised to perfection." Ainsley calls him "neatly packaged." He has his own standards and must strictly adhere to them. According to Horney, a perfectionist achieves "behavioristic perfection" and insists upon others "living up to his standards of perfection and despises them for failing to do so" (NHG, p. 196). Peter, therefore, cannot tolerate the lack of control of Marian. He cannot understand her rebelliousness and does not understand her.

The breakdown of their relationship and with it the blow dealt to Marian's predominant solution expose her to terrible inner conflicts. With her real centre not at her command, Marian is torn by strange turmoil within and without. Her inner dictates come out with many exhortations: she should be a sensible wife, she should accept life. She should follow Peter blindly, she should not show rage, should not be involved with anyone. This is the "tyranny" of her shoulds which along with her neurotic claims on the outside world generates severe inner conflicts. Problems multiply when her neurotic claims make unreasonable demands on others, insisting that all must attend to her. When they fail to follow her unuttered dictates, she is disillusioned with her friends. Her own failure to control her rage generates fear, its reaction is the anger of frustrations.

Self-hate is the logical outcome of this situation. The conflict between Marian's pride system and her real self generates a war between the healthy and neurotic forces, between constructive and destructive elements. Karen Horney terms it "central inner conflict" (NHG, p. 112). Marian oscillates between an expansive and a self-effacing view of herself, human nature and human world. Her vacillations and confusions are reflections of her inner conflicts. She will never arrive at a clear idea as long as her personality remains unintegrated. Marian shows "psychic fragmentation or compartmentalisation" which is described in psychiatric literature as a disintegrating process. In it, a neurotic fails to see himself as a whole identity and experiences himself in piecemeal which saves him from conflicts and tensions created by inner-contradictions. The function of compartmentalisation, according to Horney, is to "preserve the status quo, to protect neurotic equilibrium from collapsing" (NHG, p. 180). Quite unawares, she experiences herself in fragments. For example, on the one hand she cherishes her image: Peter's image of what she should be. On the other hand, she is a rebel, feeling one with Duncan and sees him as her other self. Marian justifies her relationship, which "according to her standards" is "perfectly innocent." "After all, we're getting married in two months" (EW, p. 189), she justifies. By closing herself to reality she resolutely follows her fantasy. By participating in Duncan's world of fantasies, she keeps herself immune from the onslaught of her self-loathing.

Marian does not have a healthy person's concept of freedom. She resorts to the "mechanism of escape," as Erich Fromm terms it, to attain freedom from conflicts. Fromm points out that this mechanism is not conducive to integrity and self-realisation. Rather, it is an escape from an unbearable situation and is characterised by its compulsive character. She runs to Duncan to evade reality. His cynicism, "You know, I don't even really like you very much," (EW, p. 183) and his complete self-centredness are very reassuring to her in her situation when she is running from involvement. She does not find her life threatened whenever she is with Duncan. Here she is caught in an "eddy of present time: they had virtually no past and certainly no future" (EW, p. 184). Duncan's fantasies provide her the escape she is seeking from her inner conflict. Erich Fromm calls it the "other course" and writes:

> *The other course open to him is to fall back or to give up his freedom, and to try to overcome his aloneness by eliminating the gap that has arisen between his individual self and the world… It assuages an unbearable anxiety and makes life possible by reflections avoiding panic; yet it does not solve the underlying problem and is paid for by a kind of life that often consists only of automatic and compulsive activities."[13]*

The compulsive nature of Marian's attitude discloses itself in her neurotic fear of violence and noise. She gets panicky at the raised voices of Peter. She fears her inner violent tendencies. The frustration of her claims intensifies her feeling of vulnerability and pushes her in the direction of expansive attitudes and values. She feels betrayed by Peter and even Ainsley and others. She has mothered Ainsley, and has looked after all her needs at home. Even she turns up in Plaza to manipulate Len into marriage. She feels psychologically responsible for Len who has allowed himself to be "led flower garlanded to his doom," he has also let her down. He had turned into a "white grub suddenly unearthed from its burrow (EW, p. 160). The control imposed upon her impulses and feelings is let loose; fear disrupts her mental equilibrium. She confesses that she is consumed by an irrational fear.

> *An irrational dread because for one thing there was no reason, she told herself… She would be safe; but what she really seemed to fear was the destruction, not of anything in her relationship with Peter, but of one of the two by the other; though who would be destroyed by whom or why, she couldn't tell, and most of the time she was surprised at herself for having such vague premonitions (EW, p. 185).*

Tortured by self-accusation and stricken by unnamed and irrational terror, Marian goes through the inner hell of self-contempt and self-torment. Marian's crisis reaches a critical point when she identifies herself with the edible commodity. She fears herself being devoured, hence, she is unable to eat. She unconsciously transfers her sympathies from the eaters to the things that get eaten. She becomes aware of what happens to things that allow themselves to be eaten. "You look delicious." "Very appetizing. And that's what will happen to you: that's what you get for being food" (EW, p. 270). Her denial of food and meat becomes "reminiscent of the deaths of early Christian martyrs" (EW, p. 155). This denial is meant to cause her to suffer continuously. Horney calls it "Schaden-feude" i.e., vindictive satisfaction at the self-inflicted pain. Marian's decision to give up food is interpreted differently by different scholars. Jerome H. Rosenberg calls it "anorexia nervosa"[14]. To another critic, food metaphorically becomes the "subconscious rejection of the victim-wife role of being consumed and assimilated by Peter."[15] It is Duncan who relates her inability to eat to an "inner rebellion." According to him, she is a representative of modern youth, rebelling against the system.

Ironically, Duncan whom Marian seeks as a sort of escape becomes the starting point of her perception. She symbolically meets her other self. Atwood reinforces the intended symbolism by making Duncan categorically emphasise the similarity between him and Marian: "you look sort of like me in that" (EW, p. 144). What differentiates the two, however, is that whereas Duncan only self-consciously plays the role of victim and works out the strategy of his dependence complex to exploit others, Marian is actually a victim and exploited by others. She is able to see herself as she is and not as seen by others. Duncan functions to reflect Marian's passivity and powerlessness. They are being exploited by others. This confrontation with the other self, analogous to the Jungian archetypal Margaret Laurence employed in her novels, sets in motion the process of self-examination and reappraisal of herself in relation to others. M. F. Salat refuses to accept the archetypal interpretation. He sees the ironic and periodic intent in the text. He agrees that "Marian descends, but to the depth of ignominy and confronts not the Shadow Self but a shady self."[16] Whether Duncan is alter ego or a shady self can be debatable but there is no doubt that he plays a significant role in Marian's fictive journey towards achieving self-hood in relation to herself as well as to the world around her. It enables her to examine the self-damaging implications and consequences of her passive acceptance of these power structures and gender roles. Marian's self-created illusion of helping "innocent" and virginal Duncan collapses and with it, her ideal image of starched nurse is also shattered. She discovers that Duncan's pose as a virgin was faked, it was, in fact, a ploy to seduce and sexually exploit her. She is not the first woman and sexual encounter with her "was fine; just as good as usual" (EW, p. 264). This revelation does not devastate her. Literally and figuratively Duncan shows Marian a way "how to get back" from his fantasy world where she has "escaped" with him to the real world of express ways. After reaching the real world, she is sure that she is going to make a decision.

In between also, we have a glimpse of her willingness to act after powder-room collapse and subsequent Plaza escapades but it is on a verbal level only. But when she sees her reflection in the mirror she feels that something has to be done in reality to stop this lack of resolve. Earlier on she identifies herself with three dolls and sees herself reflected in these dolls. Now in the bath tub, she perceives herself differently and it intensifies her fear that she would disintegrate if she does not do something about it. "All at once she was afraid that she was dissolving, coming apart layer by layer like a piece of cardboard in a gutter puddle" (EW, p. 218). All this was only at an unconscious level. Till the night of Peter's party, Peter continues to reshape Marian according to his own image of her. To measure herself "to his expectations," Marian plans to "have something done with her hair" and buy a dress "not quite so mousy as any she already owned." Though they meet with Peter's approval "Darling, you look absolutely marvellous... And I love you especially in that red dress" (EW, pp. 228, 231), Marian finds them oppressive. She experiences herself as "simply vegetable" and is overwhelmed by an obsessive fear of disintegration.

Two events bring Marian's subconscious rejection of victim-role to the conscious level. One is Duncan's frank question, "You didn't tell me it was a masquerade... Who the hell are you supposed to be?" (EW, p. 239). Marian realises that what she has so far believed to be an ideal image is nothing but a masquerade. She has lost her identity and in return, has got only an inauthentic appearance. And when Peter approaches her with camera she feels threatened; fears of disintegration grip her completely. She perceives Peter's attempt to photograph her in that guise, a threat to her real self. As a time traveller when she looks into the corridor of future life, she finds herself missing from Peter's life. John Moss in *Sex and Violence* explains Marian's fear of being photographed. According to him, "a camera can steal the soul... Identity is clearly a complex living thing. A static literal image... on film destroys intrinsic vitality and dimension, the qualities ultimately defining the soul, which is thereby lost."[17] Fearing that she in a red dress is a perfect target, she identifies Peter with the hunter and herself as a stalked victim. When she runs for her very life, she rejects the image of woman which she has allowed Peter to impose on her. When she runs from Peter, Duncan seems to her "only solid achievement... something she could hang on to" (EW, p. 263). But she faces denial from Duncan that he has "done away with her." She is no more his "illusion;" "you aren't an escape any more, you're too real" (EW, p. 258). He completely refuses to assist her to deal with Peter:

> *Don't ask me, that's your problem. It does look as though you ought to do something. Self-laceration in a vacuum eventually gets rather boring. But it's your personal cul-de-sac, you invented it, you'll have to think of your own way out (EW, p. 264).*

This comes as a powerful jolt to shake off her passivity and crumble down the cardboard world of her fantasies. Marian is neither angry nor devastated when the starched nurse like image of herself crumbles "like wet newsprint." She is not disillusioned when Duncan refuses to satisfy her neurotic claims; "it didn't make that much difference" she confesses. When seen from Maslowian angle, her behaviour is understood. Maslow observes that when our exemplary self-image which makes over-perfect demands on ourselves and others "breaks down under insight,"[18] it liberates the forces of spontaneous growth. So far, Marian's vision of world was disoriented. This insight gives her subjective and objective awareness which so far was blurred. Now she is alone but not vulnerable. She has insight and self-perception; she is strong, resolved and ready for the self-actualisation of her core. Her perception has become clear towards the final act of baking a cake which she offers to Peter as a woman's substitute. It symbolises her having the necessary self-knowledge. Henceforth, it implies she will not be Peter's (or anyone's for that matter) consumable commodity. Marian in this symbolic act of self-assertion finds a release from what George Woodcock in a nice turn of phrase calls "emotional Cannibalism."[19] Marian is finally able to defy Peter's image of herself as a perfect female with a mindless body. The cleansing mania she displays in the final section of the novel, metaphorically signifies her renewal and reformation, although it seems to her "miraculous" that she has "attempted anything so daring and had succeeded" (EW, p. 280). A scholar points out that after baking a cake for Peter, Marian is restored to her physical and mental health. She speaks in the first person singular which the critic feels is "a new and confident voice of a distinct being."[20] What the critic maintains from a feminist angle can well be applied to our discussion here. Marian shows self-confidence in her self-assertion. The novelist has presented and assessed different ways of understanding a woman's psyche and has also tried various alternatives, integrating them in the main action of the novel. Marian is present throughout the dramatisation either as an observer or as an active or passive participant. She is put to strenuous tests. After she undergoes various compulsive drives, her vision clears and she achieves a new consciousness of her self. The rhetoric is built up in favour of Marian's vindication but the mimesis leaves us open to doubt if the protagonist could really achieve transfiguration after being under the impact of self-alienating forces. However, when we explore Marian's psyche we realise that the end commensurates with the rhetoric and Marian's evolution is consistent with the rhetoric and mimesis of the novel.

A scholar emphasises the negative connotation of the circular structure of the book and maintains that Marian returns to the "point from which she began."[21] To another critic, "the novel's closing image is unsettling."[22] These scholars overlook the positive elements in the conclusion. Atwood contends that baking a cake is "an action" which "until that point she has been evading, avoiding."[23] Lauber extends Atwood's reading and sees Marian's action symbolically. To him it "represents her unwillingness to be eaten." Atwood herself acknowledges that ideal would be "neither be a killer or a victim, who could achieve some kind of harmony with the world, which is productive or creative... although not actualized in *The Edible Woman*... it's seen as a possibility finally whereas initially it is not."[24] In fact, Marian has finally been able to refuse to be *The Edible Woman*.

This fictive journey of Marian from an adopted posture of self-effacement to self-assertion is deconstructed by Atwood by using the narrative mode in which the journey motif is skilfully structured. It not only provides a map to her progressive evolution but also shows every single change in her attitude. The first twelve chapters are in first person narration and are not camouflaged by lies as in the case of the protagonist of *Surfacing* (which will be discussed later). It reveals Marian's story as candidly as the first person narrator of Kamala Markandeya does in her novel *Nectar in a Sieve*[25]. Marian's loss of the inner autonomy and self is accompanied by loss of the first person singular voice. Her story is narrated in the third person throughout Part II. The loss of individuality is indicated by the silencing of the inner voice of ironic commentary. The last chapter returns to the first person point of view to imply a rediscovery of herself. "Now that I was thinking of myself in the first person singular again, I found my own situation much more interesting than his" (EW, p. 278).

The shift in narrative strategy, from first to third person or vice versa gives the author more freedom to tell the story convincingly. I have here, Anita Desai's *Cry, the Peacock*[26] in mind where the first and last chapters are in the third person point of view; the entire novel, encompassed in between, is told by the first person narrator. Another work that can be cited is Shashi Deshpande's *The Dark Holds No Terror*.[27] Deshpande adopts the style of telling the story alternately in the first and third person. These references are not given to work out any comparison with Atwood's novel under discussion, but to establish the point that while the first person narrator helps us to understand him/her subjectively, the third person point of view gives us an objective view. What the implied author wants to portray can thus be worked out by reading between the lines.

The psychology of the characters, the events and the setting in *The Edible Woman*, coalesce with mirror imagery radiating through the narrative. The novelist highlights the theme of the novel with the help of the central metaphor: that of a woman as food. The end signals for her an emergent independent sense of self. This is her moment of inspiration, in it she establishes a contact with her authentic self. When the self flows out in the spirit of creativity and spontaneity, she grapples with her real self. Conflicts and awareness of conflicts are in themselves a sure sign of relative health. To some scholars, her presenting the woman substitute has done nothing to resolve her conflict. A reader points out that the "heroine ends where she began."[28] However, her encounter with Peter does contribute towards the resolution of her crisis. She has been obsessed with wrong. She was eaten up with anger. She has shown aggressiveness. She has a vindictive triumph and is no longer bugged. This has enabled her to get free of Peter, and she is also free from the need to be needed by Duncan. She has won a tremendous victory. She is proud that she has managed to do it. We do not contend that Marian has achieved transformation overnight. Atwood has only shown that signs of self-assertion after a period of tormenting self doubt can lead to release of tension. It remains to be seen how Atwood's heroine progresses in her second novel, *Surfacing*. It may be clarified here that the unnamed heroine of *Surfacing* is not a sequel to Marian, but an independent creation. She, too, is an alienated character who, to an extent, gets over her crisis. The next chapter of this study focuses on her.

References

1. Wayne Fraser, *The Dominion of Women* (New York: Greenwood Press, 1991), p. 119.

2. Annette Kolodny, "Margaret Atwood and the Politics of Narrative," in *Studies on Canadian Literature*, p. 92.

3. Christine Gomez, "From Being an Unaware Victim to Becoming a Creative Non-Victim: A Study of Two Novels of Margaret Atwood", in *Perspectives on Canadian Fiction*, p. 76.

4. Shannon Hengen, *Margaret Atwood's Power*, p. 48.

5. Ibid.

6. Anita Desai, "*Bye-Bye, Black Bird* (New Delhi: Orient Paperbacks, 1971).

7. S. S. Anant "Conflict Resolution through Belongingness," *Manas*, 26, Nos. (1-2), (1979), pp. 63-64.

8. Shannon Hengen, *Margaret Atwood's Power*, p. 47.

9. M. F. Salat, "A Delicious Fare: Margaret Atwood's, *The Edible Woman*," in *Perspectives on Canadian Fiction*, p. 96.

10. Linda Hutcheon, *The Canadian Postmodern* (Toronto: Oxford University Press, 1988), p. 12.

11. Coomi S. Vevaina, "Wastelanders in This New Gilead: An Analysis of Margaret Atwood', *"The Handmaid's Tale"* in *Ambivalence: Studies in Canadian Literature*, ed. Om P. Juneja and Chandra Mohan (New Delhi: Allied, 1990), p. 235.

12. Margaret Atwood, *Survival*, pp. 36-42.

13. Erich Fromm, *Escape from Freedom* (1941; rpt. New York: Holt, Rinehart and Winson, 1964), pp. 140-141.

14. Jerome H. Rosenberg, *Margaret Atwood* (Boston: Twayne, 1984), p. 99.

15. Christine Gomez, *Perspectives on Canadian Fiction*, p. 82.

16. M. F. Salat, *Perspectives on Canadian Fiction*, p. 100.

17. John Moss, *Sex and Violence in the Canadian Novel: The Ancestral Present* (Toronto: McClelland and Stewart, 1977), p. 142.

18. A. H. Maslow, *The Farther Reaches of Human Nature* (Harmondsworth, Middlesex: Penguin, 1971), p. 117.

19. George Woodcock, "Margaret Atwood: Poet as Novelist," *The World of Canadian Writing: Critiques and Recollections* (Vancouver: Douglas and McIntyre; Seattle: University of Washington Press, 1980), p. 153.

20. T. N. Dhar, "First Person Singular: The Raised Feminine consciousness in Atwood's *The Edible Woman*," *Feminism and Recent Fiction in English*, ed. Sushila Singh (New Delhi: Prestige, 1991), pp. 268-276.

21. Sherill Grace, *Violent Duality*, p. 94.

22. Pamela S. Bromberg, "The Two Faces of the Mirror," *Margaret Atwood: Vision and Forms*, p. 20.

23. Graeme Gibson, "Dissecting the Way a Writer Works," *Margaret Atwood: Conversations*, p. 15.

24. Graeme Gibson, *Margaret Atwood: Conversations*, p. 17.

25. Kamala Markandeya, *Nectar in a Sieve* (1955; rpt. New Delhi: Jaico, 1956).

26. Anita Desai, *Cry, The Peacock* (New Delhi: Hind Pocket Books, 1963).

27. Shashi Deshpande, *The Dark Holds No Terror* (New Delhi: Penguin India, 1980).

28. Linda Sandler, "Interview with Margaret Atwood," The Malahat Review, 41 (January, 1977), p. 14.

CHAPTER 3

Surfacing

The unnamed narrator of *Surfacing* comes back to her home in Northern Quebec after a gap of nine years in search of her father, who is reported missing mysteriously. The protagonist is working as a commercial artist. The reason for the deliberate separation from her parents is that the heroine was in love with her art teacher, who exploited her innocence. Against her wishes, he got the pregnancy terminated. Unable to cope with this painful reality she gave her parents a different version. She wrote a postcard and informed them that she was married, had a child and lost him to the husband whom she divorced. She invented for herself a different reality which was more acceptable than the actual one and "had come to believe the fantasy of a female adulthood constructed for her parents' benefit and had repressed the real story."[1] To some critics, the narrator's search for her missing father typifies and constitutes the essentially Canadian attribute not to disown one's parents and emblematises her desire to recover the holistic sense of self by relating herself to her origins and roots and thereby escape from being what Atwood calls "free floating citizen of the world"[2]; while to Valerie Broege, Atwood's *Surfacing* contains an analysis of "American psyche". Broege sees the narrator as a "representative of the Canadian psyche, feminine, passive, lacking identity and suffering a victim complex."[3] In Alan Twigg's words, the novel positively "reflects society."[4] Some readers point out that Margaret Atwood has dealt with Canada as a collective victim. This is affirmed by Atwood, "what I'm really into in that book (*Surfacing*) is the great Canadian victim complex."[5] Marilyn Yalom believes that *Surfacing* presents "the chaos of the unconscious." Since the protagonist is an artist, Russel Brown sees in it "implications of the artist in the myth-making process."[6]

It is clear that this unnamed protagonist has a problem with the past, and that is affecting her psyche. Since it is a first-person narration and the author does not say anything about the character by way of authorial intrusion, most of what the narrator says is tempered by the narrator's own ideas. The narrator is, therefore, unreliable. Yalom is right in saying that the narrator has "constructed a fabric of lies… so as to seal over the painful ugliness of a truth rejected by her psyche" (pp. 76-77). The novel's technique also requires an objective standpoint from which to view her. She is terrified of the past and strives to shut out the agony of experience. Her life follows a pattern of self-alienation of a severe kind leading towards her neurosis. Horney's theory provides the key to understand how the narrator's self withers and how her contact with the outside world recedes, leaving the core of her integrity impaired. From Horneyan psychoanalytical angle, the protagonist adopts the strategy of withdrawal to escape her conflicts. A deeper probing will show the psychological causes behind the dislocation of her psyche.

The chief thing needed for a proper appreciation of the protagonist's character is the psychological understanding of her motivation and the key to it lies in comprehending her divided self. Her tense and conflicted relation with the past has problematised her perception and she feels like a "Woman sawn apart in a wooden crate" (S, p. 102). Abortion and her husband's lack of support are the fountain-head of her neurosis. She calls the abortion an accident, "only with me there had been an accident and I came apart" (S, p. 102). The event had left the protagonist a psychic wreck, "emptied, amputated." Describing the devastating effect of abortion on a woman's psyche, Atwood has displayed a superb and penetrating awareness. A scholar remarks, "The trauma of abortion has never been dealt with such an extraordinary understanding before in fiction."[7] The heroine could not forget the memories of this traumatic experience. They are so real and alive that she remembers the "criminal hand" of the non-nurse, the whispers and its clinical details. It affected her later life completely in addition to what it did to her psyche. She herself confesses that she could never be the same again. Her refusal to accept "that mutilation, ruin I'd made" (S, p. 137) created intra-psychic and interpersonal conflicts. It crippled her relationship with Joe to such an extent that she could never think of marriage, and as for having a child, she is emphatic, "After the first I didn't ever want to have another child" (S, p. 47). One inner urge of human life is to create, to generate, to make alive, to bring forth something new out of the hidden treasure of being. For a woman, motherhood can lead to the satisfaction of this creative urge. In the protagonist's case, however, the abortion came as a bane and dried up her human urge for creativity.

The protagonist suffers from a very strong guilt complex which is intensified by her feeling that even unborn babies have eyes and can see like the baby in the picture "sitting up inside her gazing out...". She identifies with the unborn baby when she says, the baby was "myself before I was born...". It keeps haunting her continually and memories of it often get mixed up. She would have managed this crisis had she shown some willpower and gained the support of her ex-lover. His absence at that particular moment hurts her so much that she returns to it over and over again and always finds him missing from this agony of her experience. "He wasn't there with me. I couldn't remember why; he should have been, since it was his idea, his fault" (S, p. 74). It is not the hurt that ruins her life, it is her inability to cope with it that causes her emotional imbalance. Her solution is to stay out of it, to avoid everything and everyone. It is not a healthy person's reaction. At the time of difficulty she could enlist the support of her parents and her lover. But the heroine complicates things for herself, when in the hour of her need, she breaks ties with her parents and avoids seeing her lover. She confesses:

> After the slaughter, the murder, he couldn't believe I didn't want to see him any more; it bewildered him, he resented me for it, he expected gratitude because he arranged it for me, fixed me so I was as good as new; others, he said, wouldn't have bothered. Since then I'd carried that death around inside me, layering it over, a cyst, a tumour, black pearl; the gratitude I felt now was not for him (S, p. 139).

The heroine's anger and resentment are understandable. But what is difficult to swallow is the phobia and anxiety the incident generates. A psychologically healthy person would get over the crisis with the support of her dear ones – may be parents or husband or lover. Shashi Deshpande's Urmie, the heroine of *The Binding Vine*[8] is shattered by the death of her baby, but by and by she overcomes her trouble by getting involved in the social problem of a raped woman. Portrayal of psychic cases of women who are rived either by abortions or barrenness or death of a child abound in literature by women, be they from any country. Nella Larsen's Helga Crane, an African-American woman, for example, is psychologically disturbed when one of her many children dies. Anita Desai's Maya (*Cry, The Peacock*)[9] and Monisha (*Voices in the City*)[10] are childless. Both have a seriously injured psyche. One kills her husband in a fit of insanity while the other commits suicide on a flimsy issue. The problem with them is that they magnify ordinary situations, blow them out of proportion and succumb to self-hate. Those who have the strength to face life and its existential angst, accept the ups/downs not stoically but by being actively happy: Mulk Raj Anand's Gauri, R. K. Narayan's Savitri (*The Dark Room*[11]) or Iris Murdoch's Dora (*The Bell*[12]). It would be profitable to comprehend the conflicts of these women and to see what creates inner rift in some while others remain immune from trouble under identical external circumstances.

Discussing the problem of Atwood's heroine from a feminist angle, one critic refers to "the psychological dimensions of sexual politics which can lead a woman to the point of insanity."[13] But when interpreted from the Horneyan angle, it is different. Horney contends that a neurotic makes secret claims towards life and expects his life to be as he/she visualises it. He cannot face facts because his claims clamour, "I am something extra special" and hence, "entitled to be treated... in accord with his grandiose notions about myself" (NHG, p. 41). This includes demands made on fate also. The protagonist of *Surfacing* demands preferential treatment from her ex-lover, but finds herself alone in the hospital for abortion, which gives a blow to her "shoulds." She broods: "He hadn't gone with me to the place where they did it; his own children, the real ones, were having a birthday party" (S, p. 138). She cannot escape the pains and sufferings of a hard, harsh, protean reality. Her lover's attitude means that she is ordinary, which is beyond the scope of her neurotic claims. In these circumstances, the only significant thing is to cling to life. To come back to the everyday world means a return to knowledge. She dreads this knowledge that he is a married man. She wants to keep it locked, to forget it. Forgetting is her road to sanity and health. "A section of my own life, sliced off from me like a Siamese twin, my own flesh cancelled. Lapse, relapse, I have to forget" (S, p. 42). In her effort to forget it, she becomes an "escape artist".

The protagonist's difficulties start with abortion and the revelation of her ex-lover. His words shatter her self-image. Her self-pride forbids her to do anything with a man who is another woman's husband and had children. She cannot "accept" and hence, cannot get over her anxiety. To cope with this, she invents a less painful version of her situation. She now creates fantasies in order to present an ideal image of herself. In this realm of fantasy, she is away from pain because she is innocent and it is all the fault of her husband. Her refrain is: "I am innocent." She builds this image by fabricating lies and by twisting her memories. She remarks:

> *I have to be sure they're my own and not the memories of other people telling me what I felt, how I acted, what I said: if the events were wrong, the feelings I remember about them will be wrong too, I'll start inventing them and there will be no way of correcting it, the ones who could help are gone. I run quickly over my version of it, my life, checking it like an alibi; it fits, it's all there till the time I left. Then static, like a jumped track, for a moment I've lost it, wiped clean; my exact age even (S, p. 67).*

These lies are her neurotic needs. Tennessee Williams signifies the need of lies thus: "There are no lies but the lies that are stuffed in the mouth by the hard-knuckled hand of need, the cold, iron fist of necessity."[14] When the protagonist is trying to establish her innocence, she is showing her desperate compulsive drive. Carol P. Christ refuses to see this need, rather, he observes that she suffers from a "typical female delusion of innocence."[15] For another critic, it is not the delusion of innocence but the fact that "for the female individual to survive, she must recognize and reject not only the pathology of social and sexual arrangement but her own participation in these arrangements as well."[16] However, the fact is that the narrator projects herself as powerless and innocent, a victim of her husband's cruelties because by denying the child and withdrawing herself from all responsibility, the heroine survives the crisis and saves herself from psychological disintegration. Not only does this protect her against self-hate, it also feeds her pride. She blames her non-husband as she holds him responsible for her calamities. She does not feel the need to "explain to them why it wasn't really mine." She refuses to identify her child as her own. She blames it on him:

> *It was my husband's, he imposed it on me, all the time, it was growing in me I felt like an incubator. He measured everything he would let me eat, he was feeding it on me, he wanted a replica of himself; after it was born I was no more use. I couldn't prove it though, he was clever: he kept saying he loved me (S, p. 28).*

She feels she was used as an incubator. For her failure to cope with this clever man, she blames even her parents for not teaching her the techniques of survival in the city. For a neurotic like her, it is nothing but an act of externalisation. She feels, "I'm inoculated, exempt, classified as wounded" (S, p. 81). Externalisation in the case of the protagonist is of great significance. It not only helps her to retain her ideal image of the innocent victim of her ex-lover's cruelty but also works as a defence strategy to save her from inner conflicts and consequent onslaughts of self-hate. Emphasising the need of a posture of innocence for the protagonist, Margaret Atwood writes:

> *If you define yourself as innocent then nothing is ever your fault – it is always somebody else doing it to you, and until you stop defining yourself as a victim that will always be true. It will always be somebody else's fault, and you will always be the object of that rather than somebody who has any choice or takes responsibility for their life. And that is not only the Canadian stance towards the world, but the usual female one.*

The narrator not only defines herself as innocent but she also thinks she is powerless. By imagining herself as powerless, she feels that she is not evil. "I think, as I had no idea what I would do with the power once I got it; if I'd turned out like the others with power I would have been evil" (S, p. 31). She considers the use of power as evil. Margaret Atwood contends, "The other thing you do, if you are defining yourself as innocent, you refuse to accept power. You refuse to admit that you have it, then you refuse to exercise it, because the exercise of power is defined as evil."[18] Being an innocent, powerless and betrayed woman, she removes herself from the "inner battle field" and relieves herself of the tension by her withdrawal. In Horneyan terminology, it is a neurotic trend. In the words of Wayne Fraser, the heroine views herself "a 'nice' victim of both male aggression and American killer instinct."[19] By being withdrawn, she feels happy at her non-attachment, and happy that she has no expectations from life and from others.

Withdrawal is not new for the protagonist. Earlier in childhood she has learnt that she can escape from her inner turmoil if she frees herself from all wishes, emotional ties and efforts for winning. She glorifies her aloofness and remains stoic. Anthony Storr describes a schizoid person as cold, aloof and detached. This is "a complex mask for a repressed longing for love."[20] The narrator in childhood is not a schizoid person but the posture of her stoicity does conceal her repressed longing for love. The reason for this repression is found in her family. Paris writes that Horney assigns more responsibility to the family than to the culture for the neurosis. He remarks: "The important role Horney assigns to culture as the determinant of neuroses notwithstanding, she places more responsibility on the family."[21] According to Horney, "a child who grows up in a congenial atmosphere of confidence, encouragement in his activities and constructive discipline" develops self-confidence. Lack of this atmosphere makes the narrator "socially retarded" which she confesses is worse than mentally retarded. The protagonist's parents lacked the emotional involvement necessary for a child's growth. The protagonist's father was a botanist who "admired the eighteenth century rationalist" and the mother could enter "no emotions" in her diary. When the child is in awe of his parents' "perilous innocence," he regards them as "Gods" and develops "faith in (their) capacity to recover from anything." It is natural for a child to develop ontological insecurity and put some emotional distance between himself and others.

The protagonist has spent her childhood in the lake forest before moving to the city life. She has always felt like a stranger, a sort of alien in both environments. Being split "between two anonymities, the city and the bush" (S, p. 53), she remains alienated in both. She cannot relate to other children in the spirit of spontaneity because she is alien to their customs and religion. Her parents did not teach her religion, so she learns it as other children learn about sex. When a child does not share the fears and the defences of culture and religion, he or she has to pay, as Horney says, in *The Neurotic Personality of Our Time*, "an exorbitant price" for defences consisting in "an impairment of capacity for achievement and enjoyment."[22] Thus raised in an atmosphere far removed from realities, she can neither accept reality nor can she participate in life. It is evident in her refusal to attend the funeral of her mother. A more or less similar situation is depicted by Camus in *The Stranger*, when the hero fails to express his emotion on his mother's death. This freezing of emotion is indicative of a severed connection with the core of being.

Atwood's protagonist cannot accept her mother's death realistically, nor can she respond appropriately to that which is the reality, the ultimate end of life. She confesses later, "when she died, I was disappointed in her", she stops participating and remains bound to door knobs, fences and knots. She no longer seeks affection nor does she fight. She feels disappointed and disinterested in life. She confesses, "I was disappointed in myself: I must have been a hedonistic child, I thought, and quite stodgy also, interested in nothing but social welfare" (S, p. 85). She intuits the causes of alienation in the early stage of her childhood. The narrator recalls her childhood arguments with her brother in which she remarks:

> Fighting was wrong, we weren't allowed to, if we did both sides got punished as in a real war. So we battled in secret, undeclared, and after a while I no longer fought back because I never won (S, p. 129).

The protagonist of *Surfacing* stops playing games. This is tantamount to rejecting life as such. This fear of playing games, derives not only from her mistrust of her own capacity but also from her tendency – characteristic of neurotics – of always wanting to succeed. She cannot settle for averages, therefore, she prefers not to attempt at all. She is trying to create a special position for herself through this exaggerated refusal. To compensate for these feelings of uncertainty and inferiority, she directs her energies to becoming a "lady." She is seeking safety and her need is neurotic and urgent. She herself affirms, "'A lady' or 'A mother', either one was safe; and it wasn't a lie, I did want to be these things" (S, p. 85). She takes a neurotic pride in conforming to this image. It is reflected in her remarks, "I was civilized enough" and have become a "finished product." Feminist critics view this neurotic trend of the protagonist differently. They blame the patriarchal social system, which oppresses and treats women as the second sex. One critic argues that "the world is masculine on the whole; those who fashioned it, ruled it, and still dominate it today are men."[23]

In fact, her conformity to the social image of femininity can be attributed to the compulsion of self-destructive drives, generated by her pride system rather than to her gender. It is her search for glory which is allied to her pride system that makes her shift between withdrawal and compliance – her two major neurotic solutions.

The protagonist's flashbacks on her days with her ex-lover, reveal her compliant drives. Like ontologically insecure people, the narrator feels real, alive and whole; when she relates to her lover. He serves her psychological needs of love and belonging. Like a true compliant character she values love as the most essential part of her life. She recalls:

> *For him I could have been anyone but for me he was unique, the first, that's where I learned. I worshipped him, non-child bride, idolater, I kept the scraps of his handwriting like saints' relics, he never wrote letters, all I had was the criticisms in red pencil he paperclipped to my drawings. Cs and Ds, he was an idealist, he said he didn't want our relationship as he called it to influence his aesthetic judgement. He didn't want our relationship to influence anything; it was to be kept separate from life (S, pp. 142-43).*

It is clear that her relation with the art teacher is one of morbid dependency. She submits to his love, his demands for aborting the child. She restores her pride, dwelling on his admiration, and values his notes. She has an idealised image of him and experiences her own search for glory through him. She listens to him when he tells her that "there have never been any important women artists" and believes that "he was right, there never have been any" (S, p. 46). She even gives up the ambition of becoming "a real artist" and starts believing that "men ought to be superior" (S, p. 105). She experiences his success as her own, his glory is hers. This gives her feelings for him the neurotic intensity that makes it romantic. Horney associates it with morbid dependency. For the dependent partner in such a relationship:

> *Love must and does appear as the ticket to paradise... no more feeling lost, guilty and unworthy... love seems to promise*

protection, support, affection, encouragement, sympathy,
understanding. It will give him a feeling of worth. It will give
meaning to his life. It will be salvation and redemption.... To
love, for him, means to lose, to submerge himself in more or less
ecstatic feelings, to merge with another being, to become one
heart and one flesh (NHG, pp. 239-40).

The failure of her relationship with the art teacher deals her a
severe blow. The dismal sense of having failed produces self-
reproach and self-contempt. These, in themselves, are damaging
feelings. To save herself, the easiest way she finds is in withdrawal
and she shifts her energies to the strategy of detachment.
Withdrawal is her defense mechanism to guard her idealised self-
image as an independent individual. This elevates her in her own
eyes. She feels not only invulnerable but righteous and superior
too. The narrator's self-conscious superiority reflects in her
thoughts; she recalls that she is not "prepared for the average, its
needless cruelties and lies" (S, p. 183). Her parents "didn't teach us
about evil, they didn't understand about it" (S, p. 138). She
believes "their totalitarian innocence was my own" (S, p. 184).
These feelings become pronounced when she says that she alone
can find her father while others have failed. This appeal of
freedom is seen in her remarks about Mr Percival. She does not
like her publisher's interference in her work. She does not allow
her friends to plan the search for her father and "right now I wish
they wouldn't be here." Her behaviour matches the description
Horney gives of the difficulties faced by detached persons and
their need to be alone. The unnamed protagonist confesses, "it's
true, I am by myself, this is what I wanted, to stay here alone."
Here, the wish to stay alone is not a healthy drive of a detached,
independent person.

What she considers freedom is just a flight from conflicts. It is
a neurotic striving for resignation. It signifies a peace born out of
"absence of conflicts". In the spiritual pursuit of detachment, the
struggle is for the higher goal. Abraham Maslow terms it
"metamotivation". Hindu psychology envisages freedom from
ego involvement to the optimum degree possible. Real freedom
implies "cessation of all conflict and liberation from fear."
J. Krishnamurti points out that "unless the mind is absolutely free
from fear, every form of action brings more mischief, more misery,

more confusion."[24] The narrator is not free from fears. She is afraid of life and is closed to all its possibilities. She is afraid of Paul and his wife discovering about her. She admits "she is afraid" and in order to evade it, "I wanted to keep busy, preserve at least the signs of order, conceal my fear, both from others and from him. Fear has a smell, as love does" (S, p. 72). Thus it is seen that she experiences fear in her relationship with Joe and her friends. She is afraid that they may find about her past.

To the narrator, resignation "means giving up struggle and settling for less" (NHG, p. 260). It is a process of curtailing life and growth; wrongly does she think that she has achieved peace. Since she has not developed a healthy self-esteem, she reaches for false glory based on neurotic pride and lives in the ivory tower of her pride, safe in the belief of independence and hence her own significance. Erroneously she substitutes the real self by her actualised self-image. She blocks all consciousness. Her false self has emerged where she feels the need to give a faked version of her life. Her false self suffers from the marriage which has never existed and which the narrator calls the "paper act". She realises her glorified image of herself when she pities herself for marrying a "wrong person" and getting a divorce. "A divorce is like an amputation, you survive but there's less of you" (S, p. 36). Thus she alienates from the real self as well as from the others. C. G. Jung employs the term "self" to mean that part of a new centre of personality which includes the conscious as well as the unconscious and brings feeling of "oneness" with life – human, animal and plant. Like Horney, Atwood, in an exchange of conversation between Joe and Marian in *The Edible Woman*, terms the real self as the "Core". In *Surfacing*, the protagonist's alienation has started when she splits her life into "head" and "heart" and experiences herself as a split and divided self. She views herself as "The other half, the one locked away, was the only one that could live; I was the wrong half, detached, terminal. I was nothing but a head" (S, p. 102). Her neurotic pride system and its demands on herself alienate her from the historical present as well as from the past and more crucially from all emotions. She calls her parents "they" as if "they were somebody else's family" (S, p. 8). She realises that she has become an insensitive and unfeeling creature. "I realized I did not feel much of anything, I hadn't for a long time. Perhaps I'd been like that all my life" (S, p. 99). This is symbolised by her physical numbness; she confesses that what to feel became a kind of rehearsal for her. She recalls:

> *I rehearsed emotions, naming them: joy, peace, guilt, release,*
> *love and hate, react, relate; what to feel was like what to wear,*
> *you watched the others and memorized it. But the only thing*
> *there was the fear that I wasn't alive: a negative (S, p. 105).*

Avoidance of deeper involvement is the characteristic trait of the withdrawal type. Erich Fromm in *Man For Himself* calls it "negative relatedness." Erickson uses the term "negative identity" for the state in which "I" is burdened down, rendering an individual unable to participate in speciation. In the narrator's case "I" is not encumbered but stunted by her super-ego, her glorified image. She is sure that one can retain one's independence and sanity by closing all communication. Communication is both painful and humiliating to her. Avoidance of deeper feelings is seen in her relationship with Anna, David and Joe. Sharing and communication is difficult, both for her and Joe. It exposes her vulnerability and feelings of inadequacy. That is why she says a half-truth to Anna. When she asks about her emotional commitment, she tells her that she is married but keeps silent about the baby. "I haven't told Joe either" (S, p. 42). It is a painful reminder of her inadequacy to keep her husband when Anna could hold David.

She avoids all kinds of commitment. She loves Joe but she shrinks from marriage because it would mean emotional commitment. She wants to keep her intimacy on a physical level only. She says "Everything I value about him seems to be physical: the rest is either unknown, disagreeable or ridiculous. I don't care much for his temperament" (S, p. 51). Many critics find Atwood's protagonist sceptical of the magic word "love". Firestone observes that love between sexes is "complicated, corrupted or obscured by an unequal balance of power."[25] The cause behind this scepticism is that she is exploited and betrayed by her first lover who did say "he loved me" and the narrator will "never trust that word again" (S, p. 41). They also claim that she distrusts the word "love because for men, love is nothing but sex"… "love is taking precautions" (S, p. 74) and even Joe who is only "half formed" is no less demanding. However, it is the tyranny of the narrator's shoulds that allow her only distant or transitory relations. Therefore, she cannot allow her sexual relationship with Joe to "degenerate into love." The "shoulds" of resigned or detached people are "negative" in nature. According to Horney, they do not develop lasting relationships, they need to maintain their distance in these relationships as well. They must not show others their feelings, which ought to stay hidden, and they should not expect anything of life or other people lest they be disappointed (NHG, pp. 64-66). Their shoulds demand the repression of their needs and feelings. That is the reason why the protagonist cannot openly express her love for Joe though she feels for him. "I'm fond of him, I'd rather have him around than not; though it would be nice if he meant something more to me" (S, p. 36). It becomes comprehensible now, why the protagonist cannot express her love though she feels for Joe.

In reality, she values marriage based on love and commitment. She has respect for her parents' and Paul's marriage. "The barometer couple in their wooden house, enshrined in their niche on Paul's front porch, my ideal" (S, p. 132). Now we are in a position to understand why she says 'No' to marriage with Joe. Though her excuse is "I've tried and failed... But marriage was like playing Monopoly or doing crossword puzzles, either your mind worked that way, like Anna's or it didn't; and I'd proved mine didn't" (S, p. 81). Actually she has to protect her image of a detached person and repress any desire for intimacy and commitment.

However unfeeling, rude and alone she may pretend to be, she is essentially highly strung. She cannot tolerate other people saying that her father is dead. She reacts with vengeance. She doubts even David and feels that he is telling lies. It may be argued that even a healthy person resents criticism and injury to his pride. But there is a sharp difference between the two. A normal person's pride is based on substantial attributes of his personality such as the feeling of quiet dignity at having achieved something in life. Neurotic pride, on the contrary, stands on shaky grounds. It rests on the idealised image that she alone is capable of discovering her missing father. Therefore, the protagonist's reactions to the ordinary suggestions given by Paul or David are violent and baffle the readers. Two causes work behind these reactions. Her friends hurt her neurotic pride by being with her in her search for her father. At the conscious level she knows that she is not as self-sufficient as she glorifies herself to be and that she has to depend on them. Secondly, she is disgusted with her dependency which denotes her weakness. Thus, she alternately glorifies and scorns her independence and loneliness.

Inside, she is afraid, feels lonely and needs friends. She is happy when they are around but she shows her disregard because it is against the taboos of her withdrawal. She is caught in the crossfire of her conflicting "shoulds". She remarks; "Still I'm glad they're with me, I wouldn't want to be here alone; at any moment the loss, vacancy, will overtake me, they ward it off" (S, p. 33). She also wishes that they "weren't here. Though they're necessary" (S, p. 10). So long she has been successful in her self-deceit, considering herself immune. Till the narrator reaches the lake, whatever pain is experienced remains at the superficial level of pseudo-self. At the sight of the fish that she has killed, she discovers her vulnerability: she is not stoic, she has not done away with ties and deeper feelings and she can be touched by grief.

As Marian's crisis in *The Edible Woman* reaches a critical point when she identifies with an edible commodity, the protagonist of *Surfacing* faces crisis when she identifies with the heron. She sees her predicament in the death of heron who is killed by the Americans and strung up like a lynch victim. "Anything we could do to animals we could do to each other, we practiced on them first." It is very difficult for her to reconcile to the fact that innocents get slaughtered because they exist. In fact, it is a projection on other people of characteristics which in the course of the novel she is forced to acknowledge as her own. Incensed by the manner in which the Americans destroy the thing they have no use for, the protagonist realises "the only relation they could have to a thing like that was to destroy it." It is simply to prove that "they had the power to kill." Bellowing with pain and anger she directs her self-contempt towards the Canadians. It is a case of displaced emotions. She blames them for allowing this to happen and shows a deep indignation when she perceives an irony that it is not the Americans but the Canadians who have killed the heron. They are also becoming like them, she bursts. At this revelation, her indignation alternates with self-accusation:

> *I felt a sickening complicity, sticky as glue, blood on my hands,*
> *as though I had been there and watched without saying No or*

doing anything to stop it: one of the silent guarded faces in the crowd. The trouble some people have being German, I thought, I have being human (S, p. 124).

She admits her complicity in the killing of the heron, it brings her a deep sense of her own evil. And finally, she admits to the abortion and her guilt. She confesses "I let them catch it. I could have said no but I didn't; that made me one of them too, a killer" (S, p. 139).

This heron incident is very vital because it initiates the process of self-analysis in the case of the protagonist. She not only discovers the reason for the prevailing evil but also the hierarchy of victimisation in which the powerful gets the less powerful. She views this tendency to evil as innate: "To become like a little child again, a barbarian, a vandal: it was in us too, it was innate" (S, p. 126). We can discern a slow progress in the narrator from neurotic ego-centricity towards an allo-centric perception while analysing her own emotional bankruptcy. She perceives similar atrophy of heart in David.

David is like me, I thought, we are the ones that don't know how to love, there is something essential missing in us, we were born that way, Madame at the store with one hand, atrophy of the heart. Joe and Anna are lucky, they do it badly and suffer because of it: but it's better to see than to be blind, even though that way you had to let in the crimes and atrocities too. Or perhaps we are normal and the ones who can love are freaks (S, pp. 130-131).

Human life, says Buber, is life in dialogue and we can know the self only through it. This presupposes a communication between the consciousness of individuals. Till now, the protagonist did not have "I-thou" communication and hence, she could not develop "personal empathy." Now psychologically she begins to relate herself to other people. The relationship of Anna and David becomes worthy of her attention, which was so far outside the scope of her neurotic drives. Now she perceives Anna as a compliant character, whose marriage is not based on an emotional commitment but on a set of rules. If she breaks them, it upsets the balance. David has his own compulsions; in Horneyan terminology, his destructiveness is sadistic. He has pronounced sadistic trends because of his feelings of futility. As regards his life, there is a gap between the self and his falsely elaborated view of himself. Violence and cruelty towards Anna is an avenue of escape from his conflicts. The aggressive type does not let his victim grow independent, free from his control. This trend is seen in his relationship with Anna. When she goes on with Joe, he is jealous and possessive about her. The reality of the situation is that David does not know "how to love." He suffers from atrophy of the heart. He wishes to be loved absolutely and accuses Anna of infidelity. In fact, he is so insecure that he cannot allow Anna to be independent.

The protagonist suggests a way out of being victimised by David. She says "may be you should leave or get a divorce." As a compliant character, Anna is unable to follow the protagonist's advice. It is due to her compulsive drive and her need of David that she has "come to love" him, and is ready, though cryingly, to expose her naked body so that David can collect the sample of victims for Random Samples. In Anna's passivity and powerlessness, she not only sees a feminine passivity but her own suffering due to her morbid dependency on her ex-lover. In freeing Anna she is freeing herself. For the first time she makes an independent decision: unwinds the camera film and throws it in the lake in spite of Anna's warning to her, "You better not do it they'll kill you." She feels happy "hundreds of tiny naked Annas" are no longer bottled and shelved. In this act of freeing Anna, she has taken an action which she thought she was powerless to do. But this is a brief moment of self-discovery. She undergoes a great struggle. Her "grandiose fantasies" about herself as a detached person perish; self-hate emerges with the realisation that she has been an escape artist, expert at untying knots only; she has lacked human warmth. Her inability to share feelings with others on a human level had isolated her. Pure violence erupts as an ultimate form of introspection.

To comprehend the behaviour of the narrator, we have to explore the psychological terrain of her inner being. The narrator's state of mind is "disjointed, chaotic and restive". The narrator loses her own reality and participates in shamanic rites. She sees Amerindian river Gods, and different native Indian visions in which her parents appear as birds and animals. In Laing's terminology she is showing psychotic alienation. "When the 'self' becomes more and more participant in phantasy relationships, less and less a direct participant in real relationships, in doing so it loses its own reality."[26]

According to Joseph Campbell, these are symptomatic of her unconscious fears and tensions. Like other psychoanalysts – Jung and Freud, Campbell sees the correlation between the logic of myths and dreams. In *The Hero with a Thousand Faces*, he points out the psychological significance of these mythological and legendary heroes for the modern man. To him, it is a "symbolic expression", "given to the unconscious drives, fears and tensions that underlie the conscious part of human behaviour."[27] Erich Fromm stresses the importance of this primitivism in man's search for himself. According to him, "these are primitive systems such as animism and totemism in which natural objects or ancestors represent answers to man's quest for meanings."[28] To an ordinary onlooker, these visions are hallucinatory or mental abrasions but a scholar sees in it a "religious ecstasy."[29] These mental abrasions in case of the narrator are the ghost of her psyche, that is why Atwood calls this novel a "ghost story". By confronting these ghosts, she traces her father's sanity and possibility of his death by drowning. In these mental abrasions, she has gone only that far, and it was possible for her to come back. Her father's death symbolically represents the spiritual death of self. Her pushing herself "reluctantly into the lake" is an image that serves as a metaphor to reveal the protagonist's incipient descent into the self to discover within her psyche the split between head and feelings.

The discovery of her dead father gives her the transformative power and the illumination that "Gods of the head" are not enough for her quest for herself. Her mother's gift: a childhood painting of mother and child becomes her guide to matriarchal perception. Now she perceives that everything is alive, everything is waiting to become alive with this maternal power. She rejects her passive innocence, rediscovers her consciousness and regains her essential nature as a woman. She gives up the old belief that she is powerless and takes responsibility for her decision and her life. "I have to recant, give up the old belief that I am powerless and because of it nothing I can do will ever hurt anyone" (*S*, p. 185). Erich Fromm opines that when a man accepts his power and uses it, he can make his life meaningful. Man must accept responsibility for himself and for the fact that only by using his own powers can he give meaning to his life.

Only if he recognizes the human situation, the dichotomies inherent in his existence and his capacity to unfold his powers, will he be able to succeed in his task: to be himself and for himself and to achieve happiness by the full realization of those faculties which are peculiarly his – of reason, love and productive work.[30]

The split in this divided self gets healed when she accepts her duality and becomes free from it. Sherill Grace observes, "it is not duality but polarization that is destructive and freedom comes only when the dualities are accepted."[31] She is healed when she accepts her both halves.

Her acceptance of both halves – head and feeling is evidenced in the act of turning the mirror around. She views herself "a natural woman... a new kind of centerfold." She gives up withdrawing because now she can face life without any defenses. "Withdrawing is no longer possible and the alternative is death" (S, p. 185). She decides to "prefer life" (S, p. 182) and discovers that "feeling was beginning to seep back into me". She does not need to stay as the centrefold but makes a move towards people. Now she realises that it was not "the men" she hated but "the human beings, both men and women" (S, p. 148) "who represent evil." In the beginning of the novel she considered the possession of power as evil but now her vision is clear and she is aware that evil can be "dealt with, stopped and predicted." She feels that evil is not confined to Americans only, it is innate in us. With our power, we can stop it.

With this new found power, she is ready to face the demands and questions of Joe who has returned to the island. She is fully herself and fully human as Marie Francoise Guedon views her. Guedon says, "The heroine comes back from her dive into wilderness to re-possess herself, her memory, her normalcy. She has gained acceptance of herself and reality. She is now fully herself and fully human."[32] She accepts the humanness of her parents. She acknowledges that they are not Gods, "they dwindle, grow, become what they were, human" (S, p. 183). In accepting their humanness she frees herself from the cruelties of her false self. She accepts her humanness with her frailties and subsequent guilt.

Now she gains the ultimate sanity. According to Rigney, now "to the protagonist belongs the ultimate sanity; the knowledge that woman can descend and return – sane, whole, victorious."[33] The symbolic conception towards the end indicates the rebirth of her aborted child and signals the beginning of the process of her becoming whole again. "The two halves clasp interlocking like fingers." Rigney views in it the possibility of 'self-actualization' (S, p. 119). The narrator feels there is "No total salvation, resurrection" (S, p. 183), but Atwood writes "the heroine of *Surfacing* does not end where she began."[34] She sees the possibility of actualisation for her.

Though we have no reason to refute what Atwood says about her heroine (for, she is her creator), we have our doubt regarding her self-actualisation. The unnamed protagonist is a brilliantly documented figure having her motivational system and operating within a value-system she has lived in. The positive streak in her character shown at the end is generally interpreted as her healthy vision. But, it must be remembered that prior to the end, the heroine has discovered the cause of her father's death. With this discovery, the period of uncertainty and mental tension is over. Relieved of tension she sees life as worth accepting. She reconciles with its ups and downs.

It is difficult to accept that the protagonist who has harboured anger, frustration and defeat for long and had not even undergone any self-analysis can really become a self-actualising individual within a short time. However, we can grant her healthy vision and appreciate her decision to go back to normal life. This acceptance is found in Anita Desai's Sita in *Where Shall We Go This Summer?* which reveals the guts to face life and reconcile with it. There are others who run away from life: Kate Chopin's Edna (*The Awakening*)[35] and D. H. Lawrence's the woman who rode away. At least, Atwood lets her heroine confront facts, "to survive with dignity."[36] She achieves integration and becomes whole after experiencing fragmentation. Probably she paves the way for her next prototype, Joan Foster, who will be discussed in the next chapter, dealing with *Lady Oracle*.

References

1. Marilyn Yalom, *Maternity, Mortality and the Literature of Madness* (London: The Pennsylvania State University Press, 1985), pp. 76-77.
2. Margaret Atwood, *Second Words* (Toronto: Anansi, 1982), p. 113.

3. Valerie Broege, "Margaret Atwood's Americans and Canadians," *Essays on Canadian Writing*. No. 22 (Summer 1981), pp. 122-23.

4. Allan Twigg, *Margaret Atwood: Conversations*, p. 126.

5. Graeme Gibson, "Dissecting the Way a Writer Works," in *Margaret Atwood: Conversations*, ed. Earl G. Ingersoll (Ontario Review Press, 1990), p. 13.

6. Russell M. Brown, "Atwood's Secret Wells," in *Essays on Canadian Writing* No. 17 (Spring 1980), pp. 5-43.

7. Sushila Singh, "Joyce Carol Oates and Margaret Atwood: Two Faces of the New World Feminism," *Punjab University Research Bulletin*. Vol. 18, No. 1, 1987. p. 80.

8. Shashi Deshpande, *The Binding Vine* (New Delhi: Penguin, 1993).

9. Anita Desai, *Cry, the Peacock* (New Delhi: Hind Pocket Books, 1963).

10. Anita Desai, *Voices in the City* (New Delhi: Orient Paperbacks, 1968).

11. R. K. Narayan, *The Dark Room* (1938; rtp. ND: Orient Paperbacks, 1978).

12. Iris Murdoch, *The Bell* (London: Chatto and Windus, 1958).

13. Iqbal Kaur, *Margaret Atwood's Surfacing: A Critical Study* (Chandigarh: Arun Publishing House, 1994), p. 17.

14. Tennessee Williams, *27 Wagons Full of Cotton and Other Plays* (New York: New Directions, 1953), p. 71.

15. Carol P. Christ, "Margaret Atwood: The Surfacing of Women's Spiritual Quest and Vision," *Sings: A Journal of Women in Culture and Society*, No. 2 (Winter 1976), pp. 316-30.

16. Barbara Hill Rigney, *Madness and Sexual Politics in the Feminist Novel: Studies in Brontë, Woolf, Lessing and Atwood* (Wisconsin: University of Wisconsin Press, 1978), p. 12.

17. Graeme Gibson, "Dissecting the Way a Writer Works," in *Margaret Atwood: Conservations*, ed. Earl G. Ingersoll (Ontario, Ontario Review Press, 1990), p. 13.

18. Graeme Gibson, pp. 14-15.

19. Wayne Fraser, *The Dominion of Women*, p. 126.

20. Anthony Storr, *Human Aggression* (New York: Atheneum, 1968), p. 85.

21. Bernard J. Paris, *Karen Horney: A Psychoanalyst's Search for Self–Understanding* (New Haven and London: Yale University Press, 1994), p. 115.

22. Karen Horney, *The Neurotic Personality of Our Time* (New York: Norton, 1937), pp. 25-26.

23. Simone de. Beauvoir, *The Second Sex*, Trans & ed., H. M Parshley (London: Penguin Books, 1949), pp. 278-298.

24. J. Krishnamurti, *Beyond Violence* (London: Victor Gollancz, 1973), p. 24.

25. Shulamith Firestone, *The Dialectic of Sex: The Case for Feminist Revolution* (New York: William Morrow, 1970), p. 130.

26. R. D. Laing, *The Divided Self* (London: Penguin, 1969), p. 141.

27. Joseph Campbell, *The Hero with a Thousand Faces* (1949); rpt Princeton: Princeton University Press, 1973), p. 256.

28. Erich Fromm, *Man For Himself* (Great Britain: Routledge and Kegan Paul Ltd., 1949), p. 47.

29. Wayne Fraser, *The Dominion of Women*, p. 133.

30. Erich Fromm, *Man for Himself*, p. 45.

31. Sherill Grace, *Violent Duality*, p. 3.

32. Marie Francoise Guedon, "*Surfacing*: Amerindian Themes and Shamanism," in *Margaret Atwood: Language, Text and System*, p. 106.

33. Barbara Hill Rigney, *Madness and Sexual Politics in the Feminist Novel*, p. 115.

34. Linda Sandler, *Margaret Atwood: Conversations*, p. 45.

35. Kate Chopin, *The Awakening* (New York: The Modern Library, 1981).

36. Quoted by Iqbal Kaur in "Protest Against Sexual Colonialism: Margaret Atwood's *Surfacing* and Kamala Das's *My Story*, in *Gender and Literature, ed.* Iqbal Kaur (New Delhi: B. R. Publishing Corporation, 1992), p. 200.

CHAPTER 4

Lady Oracle

While *Surfacing* is the story of the unnamed narrator, *Lady Oracle* deals with a multi-named narrator, Joan Foster. The narrator-protagonist finds herself lost in a self-created maze of impersonations and fabrications and suffers an identity crisis because she has one too many. Joan Delacourt becomes Joan Foster when she marries Arthur and pretends not to have a mind of her own; she is Louisa K. Delacourt, the author of Gothic fiction and also the super-poet and overnight celebrity who wrote "The runaway best-seller *Lady Oracle*" (LO, p. 237). In private life, she is Arthur's wife, the Royal Porcupine's lover and the Polish Count's mistress.

The duplicity-multiplicity in Joan is so internalised that the line that divides the true from the false is not only blurred but obviated too. The fabricated fictions assume a reality of their own and Joan begins to live the Gothic fictions she creates. Her romantic identification with the Gothic heroines of her own invention leads her to expect a romantic rescue by a heroic figure, until the blackmailing reporter threatens to take away her functional identities and expose her real identity. That compels her to adopt yet another fabricated identity, that of a dead Joan. Thus she acquires a surfeit of identities, all of them fictional, and ends up having no authentic or recognisable identity. Since Joan is always poised for change, some critics consider "metamorphosis"[1] as the theme of the novel. The nationalist and the feminist critics find *Lady Oracle* not "compatible with our contemporary mood of urgent and self-conscious literary nationalism."[2] Another scholar is of the view that this comic novel does contribute to the subject of national and feminine identity quest through "the protagonist's search for integration in her sense of self and also in her style of writing."[3] Joan is a writer/ artist, and art is viewed as a slow and difficult process of self-discovery. According to Erich Fromm, an "artist can be defined as an individual who can express himself spontaneously."[4] However, in Joan's case, art does not succeed in integrating the multiple facets of her fragmented being.

Joan doesn't find her "true" self through her art but instead acquires an increasing number of identities, one completely different from the other. Contrary to what most critics say that "the novel's central theme is the resolution of multiple personalities,"[5] Joan does not succeed in forming an integrated adult self. My contention is that she fails to solve her conflict too. It will not be out of place here to compare and contrast Joan with Morag Gunn, the heroine of Margaret Laurence's *The Diviners*.[6] Morag develops a definite literary voice and establishes her independence by striving to "reach out her arms and hold people" (p. 150). Unlike Morag, Joan tries to escape the tangled web of her relationship with men from several different backgrounds. She does not develop Morag's wise "passiveness," therefore, her "whole life was a tangent" (LO, p. 311). That is why one critic calls Atwood's "heroine" as a "failed version of Laurence."[7]

From the study of the novel and the critical analysis of the scholars, it transpires that Joan is basically a compliant character with strong and prominent withdrawal tendencies. She uses different strategies of compliance, aggression and withdrawal interchangeably to cope with the situation. The key to understanding Joan lies in making sense of her vacillating, inconsistent and often bizarre behaviour and in exploring if she distorts, if she rationalises and if she blocks awareness. No critic has approached the work with a psychological theory which is congruent with it and adequate to its complexities. Joan functions, of course, as an interpreter of her own experience but we have no reason to believe that her interpretations are trustworthy or that they are affirmed by the work. But by using Horneyan tenets we can make sense of Joan's multiplicity and her psychological tensions. This will help us to know why the narrator of *Lady Oracle* fragments her personality by multiplication while the narrator of *Surfacing* fragments hers by division. When we have understood the logic of that psyche, we have understood why the work is as it is.

Two forces affect Joan's psyche and cause the identity crisis. The first is her mother's attempt to shape Joan into her own notion of female identity and her refusal to let Joan develop on her own. Her highest ambition is that her daughter be "acceptable, the same as every body else's." Joan does everything to fit into the identity her mother chooses for her. Her mother is a dominating woman whose constant nagging makes Joan feel that she is not the master of her own life. These thoughts are well-expressed in her outbursts "I didn't like her. She was always trying to tell me how to run my life" (LO, p. 91). To give some scope to the mother's behaviour, we have to consider her life. She is a woman unfulfilled. The roles of wife and mother, the desire for upward social mobility for which she forces her husband into the career of an anaesthetist, have not been able to give her identity or satisfy the demands of her psyche. Mother "urges" her husband to pursue his career relentlessly. Later, she wants to be the manager of Joan's life and take credit for her success (if any) in life. Recalling her relationship with her mother, Joan remarks:

> *Our relationship was professionalized early. She was to be the manager, the creator, the agent; I was to be the product. I suppose one of the most important things she wanted from me was gratitude. She wanted me to do well but she wanted to be responsible for it (LO, p. 67).*

In fact, Joan's confusion and the traumatic sense of having no identity begin in getting a borrowed name from the American silver screen. Joan contends, "Did she give me someone else's name because she wanted me never to have a name of my own?" (LO, p. 42). The choice of this name symbolises an alien identity, the identity of an actress who is, "ambitious, ruthless and successful" and contains a blend of multiple personalities. One scholar points out that "Joan's name introduces not only the themes of multiple personality and cultural imperialism, but also the models of female identity implicit in the conflict between mother and daughter."[8] This alien name not only problematises her relationship with her mother but also sets in the forces of alienation in her ensuing life. Cude, in her psychological assessment of Joan, attributes her unhappiness in childhood to "the cruelty of the Miss Flegg School of Dance and to her ensuing conflict with her mother."[9] Joan believes that "The only way I could have helped her to her satisfaction would have been to change into someone else." Joan equates her mother with her dance school teacher. She remarks that Miss Flegg was "almost as slender and disapproving as my mother" (LO, p. 43) and she is afraid of both of them.

Joan cannot openly display her sentiments but she silently resents her mother's efforts to "make her over in her image, thin and beautiful." She appears to Joan as a "monster" because the mother who perceives her daughter as "a reproach to her, the embodiment of her own failure... which refused to be shaped into anything for which she could get a prize" (LO, p. 67) is sure to give her daughter Joan a sense of inadequacy and lack of worth which are very damaging. Her mother further saps her of her self-esteem when she asserts that a person who looked like Joan could ever accomplish anything. Joan seethes with anger and rejects her mother's demand that she should be slim and beautiful. In order to assert herself, she enjoys overeating. She refuses to be shaped in her image. It would not be out of place here to refer to an Indian English novelist who shows a similar, if not identical, crisis of psyche. Shashi Deshpande's Saru resents her mother and resolves "If you are a woman, I refuse to be one." Saru is flippant with her mother and takes secret pleasure in going against her wishes. In Atwood's novel, Joan enjoys being fat just to show a flagrant disregard for her mother.

It is interesting to note that in Margaret Atwood's *The Edible Woman*, Marian denies herself food, while in *Lady Oracle* Joan resorts to overeating. In both cases, these are their responses to the value system which, in the case of Marian, wants to reduce her to the status of a commodity and in Joan's, wants to shape her in the model of a suitable bride in the "packaged" society. According to Erich Fromm, "It is impossible to understand man and his emotional and mental disturbances without understanding the nature of value and moral conflict."[10] An analysis of the value system in which Joan lives will enable us to reach the root of the conflict.

Interpreting her actions, Joan admits that she ate to defy her mother, but she also ate from panic. Sometimes, she was afraid that she was not a real being, that she was "an accident" (LO, p. 78). The result of overeating was that she "rose like dough," she says. Fatness gave her a feeling of victory. A scholar views this over-indulgence in food as a means of "defiance and escape".[11] Judy Kopinka in her essay, "Fat is a Feminist Issue" asserts "that being fat represents an attempt to break free of society's sex stereotypes. For many women, being fat says 'screw you' to all who want me to be the perfect mom, sweetheart, maid and whore."[12] Feminist critics discern the cruelty of society inflicted on these girls [like Joan], who are enrolled at the age of seven in dance classes and who do not fit into the "sugar and spice" image. One scholar sees the "crippling emphasis the society places on the female image as a consumer item."[13] While Marian in *The Edible Woman*, conforms to the "thin and beautiful" prescription through her anorexia, Joan's rebellious obesity is a "refutation" of her mother, a "victory". Thomas points out that Joan "wins all the battles" with her mother, including the one over what clothing to buy, but it is "at the price of total alienation from self." From the Horneyan point of view, Joan appears to be overeating to pose as an independent entity. This helps her build her ideal image of an all powerful person.

In a compliant character, the aggressive tendencies are kept in check so that the character stays true to his/her ideal image. He cannot defy the dictates of his strategy, otherwise his solution of handling his problems will crumble down. In the case of Joan, her conflicting shoulds of different strategies create conflicting demands on her and she acquires multiple personalities. It is necessary to point out that Marian in *The Edible Woman*, the narrator in *Surfacing* and Morag in *The Diviners* all discover the extent to which they inculcate their society's image of femininity, but the difference between them and the heroine of *Lady Oracle* is that Joan never breaks out of her repressed state. Joan would rather "dance as a ballerina, though, faultily, than as a flawless clown" (LO, p. 286). Despite her adolescent rebellion against the ballerina image, she harbours the desire to conform to the feminine qualities of slim gracefulness. Atwood does not allow Joan to view herself as a victim of social conditioning. She sees Joan's complicity in this process. It is made clear when Joan remarks "I wanted those things, that fluffy skirt, that glittering tiara. I liked them" (LO, p. 103).

As a result she compulsively assumes a given identity and suffers in consequence, thereof, a loss of her own distinctive identity. For instance, Joan grew up as a fat girl and developed an innate desire to be slim. Her desire to be a butterfly and not a mothball in the school dance sequence metaphorically reinforces Joan's insistent desire to be what she is not and like all Atwood's heroines, she hopes for "magic transformation" (LO, p. 43). Throughout her life she was waiting for something to happen, the next turn of events. She was also seeking something she lacked.

Aunt Lou's bequest of a thousand dollars is subject to Joan's losing a hundred pounds and is, therefore, yet another imposition on Joan's identity. The necessary fulfilment of Aunt Lou's condition requires Joan to be what she is not. Joan remarks:

> *Did it mean she hadn't really accepted me for what I was, as I thought she had – that she too found me grotesque, that for her also I would not do?... she'd offered me money to get away, to escape from my mother, as she knew I wished to; but on terms that would force me to capitulate, or so it seemed" (LO, p. 121).*

This leads Joan to grow up under a very strong pressure to distinguish herself.

Joan's impressionable years create an identity crisis for her. For example, the oddness of being a fat girl made her an object of scorn and derision of her peers. This eroded her always shaky self-confidence and led her to hide her true identity. Her school fellows in Brownie met her with spiteful and merciless jibes. They played practical jokes because she was not like them. She found herself tied to ropes and behind open door knobs. "I called out to my mother who could have saved me... But she didn't do this, she went on with" her life. Her father, a victim of his wife's assault "verbal and caustic," "brought nothing and did nothing." Joan's dreams are the reflections of the strain she suffers. In dreams she feels, "she is shut out of her mother's life; this was her mother's way of punishing her." She craves for love but "I could always recall what my mother looked like but not what she felt like," (LO, p. 89). She desires small gestures of love, like holding her hands but her mother did not hold her by the hand, "there were her gloves to think of" (LO, p. 89). Her outbursts that she is alone, does not bring any show of love and intimacy from her mother. "I don't have anyone to play with" (LO, p. 79), speaks for her alienation. Feeling alone and helpless in an atmosphere where her mother was always "disapproving", she tries to cope with her anxiety by withdrawing.

Under these circumstances, Joan cannot open herself to others and entrust herself to them. She moves not only away from, but also against and towards her fellows. She tries to insulate herself from her school fellows' contempt by keeping aloof. They had discovered how easy it was to make her cry but later Joan decides not to cry at all; "I'd decided I was through crying in public, though of course I wasn't" (LO, p. 63). To escape their derision, she began to make all progress with her emotional goodies. At school, "I was doggedly friendly and outgoing… I played kindly aunt and the wise woman" (LO, p. 93). She attempts to get on friendly terms but intimacy with them was always strained and one-sided. They confided in her but she suppressed herself. She even suppressed her interest in sex and other activities which characterise a normal girl. This initiated a process of alienation not only from others but also from the self. We begin to see now the way in which Joan's contradictory trends result in inconsistency in her behaviour and lead to her alienation. A critic aptly calls this story of Joan Foster "a poignant anatomy of childhood terror and alienation."[14] She represses her need for love and seeks to fulfil other needs which have been distorted in neurotic ways. Joan terms it "Miss Flegg's Syndrome," which means "If you're going to be made to look ridiculous and there's no way out of it, you may as well pretend you meant to. I didn't learn this rule till much later, not consciously. I was wounded, desolated in fact" (LO, p. 48). Joan becomes a passive onlooker on life. This passivity entails the loss of virginity because she is too timid to say "no" to the Polish Count.

As is often the case with self-effacing people, Joan is drawn to self-assured people who have a mission in life and allow her to participate in their glory. Fromm terms it "masochistic strivings" in which an individual, in order to overcome the panic resulting from loss of identity, seeks his "identity by continuous approval and recognition by others" (*The Fear of Freedom*, pp. 177-78). Joan too moves towards the Polish Count, Arthur and the Royal Porcupine.

The Polish Count is good, 'gentle and harmless,' the Last of the Mohicans. She is attracted to him because he fulfils the demands of her idealised self. She invests him with qualities such as "daring," "having a mission in life" and so on. Physical intimacy with such a man raises her worth in her own eyes, "I was flattered by the attention he was paying to me and grateful for it, and especially I was pleased to be thought wise" (LO, p. 148). She feels normal as a woman. "It proved to me finally that I was normal, that my halo of flesh had disappeared and I was no longer among the untouchables" (LO, p. 150). When he becomes jealous and possessive, and love begins to "resemble a shark fight," she feels a "little like Eva Braun in the bunker." The Royal Porcupine loses his appeal for Joan when she discovers a conventional Edgar Linton beneath his Heathcliff pose. She leaves him and becomes involved with Arthur, who feeds her pride by showing respect for her intelligence.

That Arthur is important in her life, is reflected in her confession, "Arthur, I said was very important to me and I didn't want to do anything that would hurt him" (LO, p. 254). Winning the love of a man like Arthur, with a cause, raises her image in her own eyes. It gives her life a sense of purpose and meaning, "The right man has come along, complete with a cause I could devote myself to. My life had significance" (LO, p. 171). She is happy to belong to such a man; she describes herself as "bliss-filled" and "limpid eyed" (LO, p. 171). She is ready to devote all her life to Arthur because she needs love and security in marriage. Observing her inner processes during her sojourn in Italy, it becomes clear that she needs Arthur's love. She admits, "I didn't ask much. I only wanted to be loved." She "loved his deliberate threadbareness, his earnest idealism, his ridiculous (to me) economies... his far-sightedness" (LO, p. 168). To please Arthur is of paramount importance in her life. This is her neurotic need and she makes all efforts to fit into a new image, that of a loving and dutiful wife. Her earnestness to please Arthur is visible in her remarks: "I retreated behind the camouflage of myself as Arthur perceived me... He wanted me to be inept and vulnerable... I could permit myself to be inept and vulnerable only because I had a core of strength, a reservoir of support and warmth that could be drawn on when needed" (LO, p. 92). To this end, she serves inedible food because "Arthur enjoyed my defects... My failure was a performance and Arthur was the audience. His applause kept me going" (LO, p. 210).

Arthur's expectations were not confined to cooking only. With every change in Arthur's social concern, Joan has to adjust her views. She even adopts the posture of a kind sympathetic human being. Arthur appreciates her empathy with suffering human beings and calls it "naive humanism." She confesses, "For years I wanted to turn into what Arthur thought I was, or what he thought I should be" (LO, p. 210). To preserve this idealised image, she fits into femininity which she otherwise resents doing. "This role is forcing me into a mold of femininity that I could never fit" (LO, p. 103). But she willingly enacts this role because she lacks the strong sense of identity necessary for assuming responsibility for the direction of her own life. Unlike the liberated Morag, in *The Diviners*, who finds both independence and relatedness, Joan is constricted by her need for dependence on someone to hold her. She is afraid of Arthur's adverse judgement of she being unworthy of his love because she cannot stand losing him. Erich Fromm calls this relationship "masochistic dependence" in which both are means to an end, "both are instrumental to each other... The most important and the most devastating instance of this spirit of instrumentality and alienation is the individual's relationship to his own self... he sells himself and feels himself to be a commodity." Thus, the self-confidence, the 'feeling of self,' is merely an indication of what others think of the person. It is not *he* who is convinced of his value regardless of popularity and his success on the market. "If he is sought after, he is somebody; if he is not popular, he is simply nobody."

Joan's sense of self-significance dwindles at times when she feels that she is a non-entity for him. But her self-image rises whenever she feels that their marriage was happier than most. She confesses "I even became a little smug about it" (LO, p. 215). When Arthur's friends envy him for having such an understanding wife or when Arthur admires her, she feels gratified because Arthur's admiration always raises her idealised image. This wish to get his praise, remains with her even after she physically leaves him and crosses over to Italy. In a compliant character, the inclination to please the partner is very prominent. "I would love him to know I'd done something complicated and dangerous without making a single mistake. I'd always wanted to do something he would admire" (LO, p. 27). She wants to be a woman whose mind he could respect.

By the time of Joan-Arthur episode, Joan's basic character structure has been formed, it changes little from thereon. Along with compliance, she has strong withdrawal trends which are rather evenly balanced. They exist mainly as attitudes. Her lifestyle is determined by compliant trends: she is willing to ignore her needs to cope with Arthur's moods and anxiety but not without giving up the independence and integrity of her individual self. This show involves enormous pain to the performer/Joan. Nevertheless, for many years, Joan does not permit herself to entertain consciously the notion that her marriage is anything other than a success. As a part of this denial, she compartmentalises and suppresses a great deal of anger, resentment and frustration.

The violence of Joan's inner conflict is evident when she speaks of the absolutely opposite elements (impulses towards independence) which have been swarming her and the shoulds created by her compliant trends make it impossible for her to admit her duplicity. "It was the fact that I was two people at once, with two sets of identification papers, two bank accounts, two different groups of people who believed I existed. I was Joan Foster, there was no doubt about that; people called me by that name and I had authentic documents to prove it. But I was also Louisa K. Delacourt" (LO, p. 213), a writer of Gothic romances. These remarks make it clear that like Morag, Joan's chief personality crisis concerns her growing awareness of the disparity between her outward appearance and her inner sense of identity. Although she feels uncertain and unhappy at her multiple identities, she derives courage from the fact that some of the persons she has known all her life have had double identities. Her father, for example, was a "healer and a killer," even the Royal Porcupine had a sinister side to his personality. Such duality is a common factor with all human beings, so she contends that she is not weird. These thoughts elevate her and help her gain confidence in her work. Her Gothic romances give meaning to her life. In her search for glory she is definitely making a big leap. Her happiness is expressed by such lines as these: "I just drifted around, singing vaguely, like the little Mermaid in the Andersen fairy tale" (LO, p. 216). She finds her work meaningful, "Well, this is my work and I find it meaningful..." (LO, p. 36). She feels she is providing escape to people because she knows all about escape, she was brought up on it. Joan's justification resembles the remarks made by Janice Radway that "romance fiction offers an escape from and a means of coping with the demands of their roles as wives and mothers."[15]

In the early stages of her relationship with Arthur, she enjoyed being a Gothic romancer. "I'd always felt sly about it, as if I was getting away with something and nobody had found me out; but now it became important" (LO, p. 213). Joan's work at current costume Gothic provides a fantasy release for her. When she could spend some time as Louisa K. Delacourt, she was patient and forbearing, warm and a sympathetic listener. But if she could not work at current costume Gothic, she would become irritable, she would drink too much and start to cry. Her compliant trends make neurotic demands on her and prevent her from enjoying her triumphs. Her oscillations and confusions are reflections of her inner conflicts. It is because the moment she becomes a celebrity as the writer of *Lady Oracle*, she recoils from success. "I feel visible," she says and takes care to deflate public attention. This characteristic fits in with the description Horney gives of a neurotic. A neurotic, Horney says, cannot experience his success directly. Joan wallows in self-doubt and self-pity. "What was the use of being Princess for a day if you still felt like a toad?" (LO, p. 238), she cries, and is scared that Arthur would be humiliated by her success.

Her glorified self cannot let her admit that she is a celebrity. She also avoids the issue of having led a double life. In order to rationalise her behaviour, she takes a visible pride in both her lives. This satisfies her neurotic need to live in fantasy:

> The difficulty was that I found each of my lives perfectly normal and appropriate, but only at the time. When I was with Arthur, the Royal Porcupine seemed like a daydream from one of my less credible romances, with an absurdity about him that I tried to exclude from my fictions. But when I was with the Royal Porcupine, he seemed plausible and solid. Everything he did and said made sense in his own terms, whereas it was Arthur who became unreal; he faded to an insubstantial ghost, a washed out photo on some mantelpiece I'd long ago abandoned. Was I hurting him, was I being unfaithful? How could you hurt a photograph? (LO, p. 259).

She defends herself against her inner conflicts by adopting the strategy of compartmentalisation. "I'd always tried to keep my two names and identities as separate as possible" (LO, p. 33). This also saves her from the onslaught of self-hate and self-contempt.

This intellectualising is a form of pride-restoring device, but it is also a defense against disintegration.

Behind these rationalisations lies her self-consciousness of multiplicity. "I was triple, multiple, and now I could see that there was more than one life to come, they were many. The Royal Porcupine had opened a time-space door to the fifth dimension, cleverly disguised as a freight elevator and one of my selves plunged recklessly through" (LO, p. 246). Her problem is how to "live practically with" these dualities/multiplicities that she contains. "What *Lady Oracle* implies," says Grace, "is... that we are all double, perhaps multiple... It is learning how to live practically with this knowledge that is difficult."[16] She feels she is nothing and it results in making her a nervous wreck. She is self-alienated and the neurotic character structure which has replaced her real self has not achieved even a spurious integration. She confesses:

> *I was a nervous wreck, I realized and I'd been one for sometime... Arthur was never there, for which I didn't blame him; I'd been unfaithful to him but I didn't have the courage either to tell him or to do it again, as I wished to. It wasn't will power that was keeping me away from the Royal Porcupine, it was cowardice. I was inept, I was slovenly and hollow, a hoax, a delusion (LO, p. 251).*

Thus it is clear that Joan has tried to "learn how to live with this knowledge" but at the price of losing her real self. It is important to point out here that Joan is not true to herself. When Orwell quotes Shakespeare's maxim "To thine own self be true" (CE, I, II, p. 134), he supports the idea of a central self which exists despite the duality or plurality of impulses, and despite the ambiguity of responses. It is akin to the inviolate inner self which Winston Smith seeks to preserve in *1984*.[17] In the case of Joan, she is alienated from this central self, and this has intensified her neurosis.

However, none of her actions, impulses or values is an authentic expression of her real self. Every one is subject to immediate repudiation by the conflicting components of her defense system. She experiences a feeling of being unreal. "It was true I had two lives, but on off days I felt merely playing house, I wasn't really working at it. And my Costume Gothics were only paper; paper castles, paper costumes" (LO, p. 216). Her self-alienation gains physical and psychological dimensions when she becomes a celebrity, as the writer of *Lady Oracle*. That her alienation is at its highest is reflected in her remarks: "I feel very visible. But it was as if someone with my name were out in the real world, impersonating me, saying things I'd never said but which appeared in the newspapers, doing things for which I had to take the consequences: my dark twin, my funhouse-mirror reflection" (LO, p. 250-51). Such thoughts show her fragmentation. She is also conscious that if she brought the separate parts of her life together, there would be an explosion. So she floats, marking time, creating uncertainty which is reflected in the pattern of her relationships.

In her relationship with Arthur and the Royal Porcupine, Joan displays the many sidedness of her character. She is motivated not only by her need for love and rapport with Arthur but she also craves for self-expression which fulfils her fantasies. Julie Fenwick sees risk in these choices and views them as incompatible with a successful relationship. While analysing *Lady Oracle* and *Anne of Green Gables*, she points out that these stories share the "underlying theme of the risk to women of certain choices – to seek forbidden knowledge, to exercise creativity, to desire, to speak, to dance". In *Lady Oracle*, "dancing becomes a recurring motif for female creative freedom, and it is depicted as incompatible with a successful heterosexual relationship; 'you could dance or you could have the love of a good man'."[18] Joan undergoes tension because she is unable to choose between the two images she has of herself, the self image of good wife and that of a creative writer. Tension generates conflict as she tries to hide her past and live a present which is a product of that past. Cude's psychological assessment in "Bravo Mothball! An Essay on *Lady Oracle*" is that "because [Joan] takes her past to be ugly, she lies constantly to conceal what she cannot contemplate."[19] Thus it becomes clear that Joan's fragmentation arose largely from her need to conceal from others, particularly men, those aspects of her personality that she believed they would find unacceptable. She sees the same multiplicity in Arthur. His character structure has certain similarities to her own. Like her, he is also aloof and detached, he is not single-minded as she once thought him to be. Mentioning their similarities Joan records, "once I'd thought of Arthur as single-minded, single-hearted, single-bodied... But I soon discovered there were as many of Arthur as there were of me.

The difference was that I was simultaneous, whereas Arthur was a sequence" (LO, p. 211).

Both Joan and Arthur display marked tendencies to withdraw when there is a breakdown of the posture of self-effacement. When Joan publishes *Lady Oracle*, her friends and the literary community find her work "a very angry book" and read it as an attack on marriage. Arthur is angered and insulted by the readers' assumption that the ambiguous lover in this book is the "unflattering portrait of himself". Arthur responds by being indifferent. Joan becomes panic stricken. She resents his lack of interest and his overwhelming reactions. "It's not like him at all. He's acting as though it just doesn't exist but at the same time he's hurt by it." She does not see any justification in his hostility as her claim is that she is happy in her marriage. One critic views this as Joan's failure to rebel: "Joan's refusal to act upon or even recognize her growing impatience with Arthur is indicative of her failure to rebel against male domination."[20] As a self-effacing person, Joan cannot bear it when Arthur withdraws. His decision is tantamount to rejection and a compliant person who depends on love, cannot accept rejection. "But he'd made a decision about me finally, a pronouncement, thumbs down. I was unworthy, I would have to go, and this was his plan to get rid of me" (LO, p. 292). When all her selves threaten to overlap, escape is her ultimate resort. "I had to get away as quickly as possible." It is important to mention that escape is the salient feature of her character structure.

When she has messed up her life, escape is the only solution to her life of falsity, hypocrisy, arrogance and authority. According to Erich Fromm, an instinctive human reaction is to flee when the "vital interests" of the individual are "threatened."[21] Brought up in an environment of obedience and weakness, a really individualistic woman would feel threatened if she is reduced to a submissive and passive partner. "Escape," says Sunaina Singh, "in this sense is used by both Anita Desai and Margaret Atwood as a defense mechanism."[22] Joan is constantly on the run, getting away from her mother, her former self, Paul, domestic life, the Royal Porcupine and in the end from Arthur, her husband. She admits "the real romance of my life was that between Houdini and his ropes and locked trunk; entering the embrace of bandage, slithering out again. What else had I ever done?" (LO, p. 334). It would be appropriate here to compare this tendency of Joan with Saru in Shashi Deshpande's novel, *The Dark Holds No Terror*.[23] Shashi Deshpande's Saru runs away when she confronts the question of identity. First, she leaves her parents in defiance and anger, later when her husband seems to deny her due identity, she runs back to her maiden home. Her identity is realised only after her neighbours flock to her, and recognise her as a doctor. The question of identity here is as much feminist as psychological. That Joan runs away because no one seems to accept and acknowledge her identity is clear in her remark, "How much better for me if I'd been accepted for what I was and had learned to accept myself too" (LO, p. 103). She extricates herself not because of her impulse to change but because of her failure to make people accept her with her failings.

Confrontation and sorting out of emotional differences are difficult tasks for a compliant character. In addition, Joan realises that confrontation with some people, her mother, for example, has no effect. Her mother, a hysterical and self-righteous person, could never believe that anyone else, especially Joan, could be right. In the case of Arthur, there was no trial and no redress. Once he had made up his mind, it was his final judgement. Joan remarks about Arthur, "He never had fights with people, he never talked things out with them. He would simply decide, by some dark, complicated process of evaluation, that these people were unworthy" (LO, p. 212). It is this attitude that prompts Joan to escape rather than confront. Frank Davey, analysing Joan's difficulties in male-female relationships, remarks that she "relives her parents' drama of the unfulfilled, isolated and dependent woman linked to an aloof and undemonstrative man."[24] She chooses to escape from the overpowering sense of righteousness, aloofness and indifference of this "undemonstrative man". Whatever may be her rationalisation, the fact is that she is frightened and escape is the only defense mechanism to restore her pride and provide a semblance of order in life. "My life was a snarl, a rat's nest of dangling threads and loose ends. I could not possibly have a happy ending, but I wanted a neat one. Something terminal, like scissors. I would have to die" (LO, p. 293).

Joan is beset with feelings of fear, rage, remorse and desire but her predominant feeling is anxiety that Arthur might discover her fake suicide and her multiple lives. If he does, then her triumph (of mastering such a situation) will be lost, she will be humiliated and proved finally unworthy. If he comes as she wishes him to (that a romantic hero will come to save her from her trouble – her fantasy), it will bring reality into her retreat, where she is marooned in the realm of her dreams. But then, he will bring with him emotional demands that threaten her basic defense—withdrawal into fantasy life. When in Italy, she is again prompted to run because she is feeling lost, disillusioned. She is optimistic, "This time I really would disappear, without a trace. No one at all would know where I was, not even Sam, not even Arthur. This time I would be free completely, no shreds of the past would cling to me, no clutching fingers. I could do anything I wanted" (LO, pp. 333-34).

Barbara Godard, in her critical analysis of Elisabeth Tassy of Hébert and Joan Delacourt, remarks that both these heroines "must accept the multiplicity of their being in order to find themselves."[25] Joan is aware of this multiplicity. She sees herself playing the roles of many wives of Redmond, she knows that she has peopled her personal and fictional world with projections of her intolerable repressed selves. She shows this awareness in the final episode of the Gothic romance *Stalked by Love* when Joan takes her heroine into the centre of the maze that is occupied by four women, all manifestations of other phases of her own life. Thus "she [Joan] found herself in the central plot" (LO, p. 341). To Godard "all the female characters are the fragments of her multiple self… so too are the male characters alter egos."[26] It is important to mention here that Joan would have moved towards unity of her being by recognising her multiplicity, but she reacts to this situation in a different way. She prefers escape to any such acceptance. One scholar remarks that Joan "prefers escape into fictional versions of life (that is art) to any acceptance of the limitations of living in the reality of it."[27] Escape and fantasy are the two devices Joan makes full use of. Some intra-psychic forces behind this behaviour are suggested by Horney's description of withdrawal as a way of protecting pride. "In the long run this makes it necessary for him to withdraw farther from others…. In order to endure life he must now entrench himself more firmly in his private fantasy world" (NHG, p. 107).

For her, without fantasy there is no escape. It becomes clear in her relationship with the Royal Porcupine. He was a welcome escape. When he becomes real she wants to leave him. For her, where there is no fantasy, there is no escape. "From this soggy domestic atmosphere, the Royal Porcupine was a welcome escape. He didn't make demands; with him it was easy come, easy go" (LO, p. 257). Talking of the Royal Porcupine she says, "For him, reality and fantasy were the same thing, which meant that for him there was no reality. But for me it would mean there was no fantasy and therefore no escape" (LO, p. 270). In *The Edible Woman*, Marian finds escape in Duncan; in the case of Joan, the Royal Porcupine serves the same purpose. In her sojourn in Italy she confesses, "I was an artist, an escape artist" (LO, p. 334). But these created intra-psychic and interpersonal problems for Joan. It initiated the fragmentation of Joan's identity into a mosaic of roles which threaten to tear her apart and it intensifies her neurosis.

Perhaps the most striking indication of the severity of Joan's neurosis is the intensity of her self-hate. From the beginning to end, the narration of events is filled with incidents of extreme self-hate. Horney lists "six modes of operation in or expression of self-hate": "relentless demands on self, merciless self-accusation, self-contempt, self-frustration, self-tormenting, and self-destructive" (NHG, p. 117). All these modes are powerfully at work in Joan's life. The affair with Arthur and later with the Royal Porcupine leaves Joan overwhelmed by remorse and tortured by self-hate. She externalises her self-hate and is angry with Arthur. She blames Arthur for driving her towards Chuck.

> *Why had Arthur driven me to it, what did he propose to do about it, shouldn't we discuss our relationship to find out what had gone wrong? For some complicated and possibly sadistic reason of his own he'd allowed me to become involved with a homicidal maniac, and it was time he knew about it (LO, p. 72).*

There are times when she blames herself for her treatment of Arthur. "Some days I felt his unhappiness was all my fault, I was neglecting him. But more often I tried to dismiss it. Perhaps he simply had a talent for unhappiness, as others had a talent for making money. Or perhaps he was trying to destroy himself in order to accuse me that I was destructive. He was beginning to accuse me of not taking enough interest in his work" (LO, p. 257). She hates herself because she desperately longs for love. But she knows that she will always be cut off from it by her own nature. In her self-berating, she judges herself harshly: "I was not a good woman" (LO, p. 212), "I was deficient" (LO, p. 269). She is angry with herself, but her anger is mixed with fear. It is expressed in her outburst:

> *I was furious, but I was also frightened. He'd discovered at least two of my secret identities... I couldn't stand the thought of Arthur knowing about my previous life as Pneumatic Woman. And if he told the media people the truth about Louisa K. Delacourt, my brief interlude of being taken seriously would be over. Unpleasant as it had been, I'd discovered it was much better than not being taken seriously (LO, p. 286).*

She is overcome by self-loathing and feels that she is worthless. Except escaping she has done nothing worthwhile. She berates herself as a "Mongoloid idiot", "a fraud, liar and imposter", "hollow, a hoax, a delusion", "I hated myself for thinking this. I felt like a monster, a large blundering monster, irredeemably shallow" (LO, p. 271). She indulges in self-accusation when she says she is an "assemblage of lies and alibis." "I'd lied to him, that I'd never been a cheerleader, that I myself was the fat lady in the picture" (LO, p. 197). She accuses herself of using love for serving her ends. "I felt I'd never really loved anyone, not Paul, not Chuck the Royal Porcupine, not even Arthur, I'd polished them with my love and expected them to shine, brightly enough to return my own reflection, enhanced and sparkling" (LO, p. 282).

Though Joan has some understanding of her self-hate, there are aspects of it which puzzle her. She is puzzled by the disparity between her ideals and her actions. She not only fails to live up to her ideals but she seems compelled to violate them. Her brief affair with the Royal Porcupine begins at the moment when she feels capable of intellectual superiority, when she oscillates between "I should" and "I won't." At first she struggles in agony against her multiple life. "I would repent, I would turn a new leaf, I wouldn't call the Royal Porcupine, although I was longing to" (LO, p. 246). Then she comes to feel that it is her normal condition and finally she takes pleasure in it. The more conscious she becomes of her position, the more anxious she becomes. Cude argues that Joan uses Arthur as an excuse for her failings, a reason for not trying to improve herself as a person in her own right (p. 161). Her escapade with the Royal Porcupine is a defense against failure. It is at the same time, a punishment for failure. She cannot be aware of her ideals without also being aware of her failure to live up to them and this is bound to generate self-hate and the need for relief through self-flagellation.

In *The Adolescent Girl in Conflict*, Gisella Konopka observes that "the gap between the feminine ideal and her own reality can motivate her to seek an outlet for aggression that is linked to her feelings of acceptance as a woman. Sexual misconduct is the logical result."[28] Yet another motive for Joan's dissipation is her need to rebel against her shoulds. Being a withdrawn person, she cannot stand any form of coercion and nothing is more coercive than the tyrannical shoulds. Such people, says Horney, "may go through alternating phases of self-castigating 'goodness' and a wild protest against any shoulds. There may be a constant shuttling between "I should" and "no, I won't"… often these people give the impression of spontaneity and mistake their contradictory attitudes towards their shoulds for 'freedom' " (NHG, pp. 77-78). As we have seen, Joan's consciousness of ideals fills her with a sense of failure and activates her self-hate. "By wallowing in self-accusation and a feeling of unworthiness," Horney observes, "the masochistic person may derive satisfaction from an orgy of self-degradation."[29] This pain gives way to self-pity; pity for herself because she cannot enjoy triumph. She also wallows in hopelessness, feeling that she can never change. She is one of those "who despairing of ever being able to measure up to [their] standards have consciously or unconsciously resolved to be as 'bad' as possible." Such a person wallows in his badness "with a kind of desperate delight" (OIC, p. 204). Joan feels hopeless about resolving her problems and about living up to her shoulds. Consequently, she indulges in endless self-reproaches. Even her escape to Italy under a false identity provides her no relief. "Where was the new life I'd intended to step into," she wonders, "easily as crossing a river? It hadn't materialized and the old life went on without me. I was caged on my balcony waiting to change" (LO, p. 310).

The compliant person finds the meaning of life in love, the aggressive man finds it in mastery, for the detached person the highest value of all is freedom, independence. This can be a healthy value but as Horney points out, "the fallacy here is that he looks upon independence as an end in itself and ignores the fact that its value depends ultimately upon what he does with it. His independence, like the whole phenomenon of detachment of which it is a part, has a negative orientation; it is aimed at not being influenced, coerced, tied, obligated" (OIC, p. 77). For Joan, freedom is the goal of life, the highest fulfilment, for which she is ready to undergo fake suicide and suffer alone in order to have it. One reason why she wants freedom so much is that she possesses so little of it because of her compulsions. Her hatred for reality is in part a hatred of her own compulsions which she longs to escape. There are times when she mistakes her contradictory attitudes towards her shoulds for freedom but her rebelliousness and vacillations are themselves compulsive. She glorifies escape as an evidence of free will. Her capricious and incomprehensive behaviour is thoroughly explicable in terms of her neurosis. She prizes freedom, will, caprice, individuality and intellectual superiority; and above all she has a profound aversion towards conformity to law, ordinariness or stupidity. When her privacy is invaded or emotional demands are made of her, she walks out of this life because it preserves for her what is most precious for her individuality. But when she fails to find the desired freedom in her escape to Italy, she contemplates one more flight; this time, it is fleeing back home.

The novel is open-ended and chances are that Joan may go back to save her friends from embarrassment, or she may stay in Italy and live under the constant dread of being detected as a fake. In sum, Joan has not been able to resolve her conflicts. She appears to be going round in circles, as if caught in a whirlpool. The steps taken by the earlier two heroines towards affirmation are forestalled by Joan Foster. It remains to be seen what Atwood's protagonists, Elizabeth and Lesje, discussed in the next chapter, do to resolve their crisis.

References

1. David Stouck, *Major Canadian Authors*, p. 285.

2. Clara Thomas, "*Lady Oracle*: The Narrative of a Fool-Heroine," in *The Art of Margaret Atwood*, ed. Arnold E. Davidson and Cathy N. Davidson (Toronto: Anansi, 1981), p. 174.

3. Wayne Fraser, "Still Fighting the Same Bloody Battles As Always: *The Diviners* and *Lady Oracle*", *The Dominion of Women*, p. 150.

4. Erich Fromm, *The Fear of Freedom* (1942; rpt. London: Routledge and Kegan Paul, 1960), p. 223.

5. Wayne Fraser, *The Dominion of Women*, pp. 149-150.

6. Margaret Laurence, *The Diviners* (Toronto: Anansi, 1974).

7. Wayne Fraser, *The Dominion of Women*, p. 149.

8. Wayne Fraser, p. 156.

9. Wilfred Cude, "Bravo Mothball! A Essay on *Lady Oracle*," in *The Canadian Novel: Here and Now*, ed. John Moss (Toronto: Anansi, 1978), p. 48.

10. Erich Fromm, *Man for Himself*, p. 27.

11. Linda Hutcheon, *The Canadian Postmodern*, p. 146.

12. Quoted by Wayne Fraser, *The Dominion of Women*, p. 156.

13. T. Nagesware Rao, "Male Mapping and Female Trapping: Parodic Deconstruction in Atwood's *Lady Oracle*," in *Perspectives on Canadian Fiction*, ed. Sudhakar Pandey, p. 114.

14. Jerome H. Rosenberg, *Margaret Atwood* (Boston: Twayne, 1984), p. 112.

15. Janice Radway, *Reading the Romance: Women, Patriarchy and Popular Literature* (North Carolina: University of North Carolina, 1984).

16. Sherrill Grace, "More Than a Very Double Life," in *Violent Duality*, p. 133.

17. George Orwell, *The Collected Essays, Journalism, Letters of George Orwell*, ed. Sonia Orwell and Ian Angus, (Secker and Warbirg, 1970), 4 vols, II, p. 134.

18. Julie Fenwick, "The Silence of the Mermaid: *Lady Oracle* and *Anne of Green Gables*," *Essays on Canadian Writing*. No. 47 (Fall 1992), pp. 51-52.

19. Wilfred Cude, "Bravo Mothball! An Essay on Lady Oracle," in *The Canadian Novel: Here and Now*, ed. Moss, p. 48.

20. Wayne Fraser, *The Dominion of Women*, p. 160.

21. Erich Fromm, "Instinct and Human Passion," *The Anatomy of Human Destructiveness* (New York: Penguin Books, 1977), p. 24.

22. Sunaina Singh, "Escape as Evolution in *Lady Oracle* and *Where Shall We Go This Summer*?" in *Ambivalence*, p. 160.

23. Shashi Deshpande, *The Dark Holds No Terror* (New Delhi: Penguin India, 1980).

24. Frank Davey, "Atwood's Comic Novels," *Studies in Canadian Literature* 5 (1980), p. 214.

25. Barbara Godard, "Strategies for Subversion in Atwood and Hé bert," in *Canadian Literature*," p. 215.

26. Barbara Godard, p. 220.

27. Linda Hutcheon, "Process, Product, Politics: The Postmodernism of Margaret Atwood", *The Canadian Postmodern*, p. 147.

28. As quoted in Judith Finlayson, "More to Birthcontrol Than Mere Education," *The Globe and Mail*, August, 6, 1983, p. 4.

29. Karen Horney, *New Ways in Psychoanalysis* (New York: Norton, 1939), pp. 272-73.

Chapter 5

Life Before Man

Life Before Man is in many ways different from Margaret Atwood's works discussed earlier. Apparently, the novel focuses on the life of three characters namely, Elizabeth, Nate and Lesje and their day-to-day problems. At one level, it is a novel of social realism in which modern urban society is depicted. One critic calls it a "sombre novel of social realism" and adds that "this familiar tale of urban infidelity is Atwood's examination of the moral torpor of her generation in the late seventies."[1] Another critic opines that these lives "mirror the monotony and emptiness surrounding them," and argues that "the novel represents a new stage in Atwood's development: it is her first attempt at social and domestic realism unmediated by satire, comedy or symbolism."[2] However, Atwood's aim, it becomes apparent, is to crystallise precisely the bleak and dreary aspects of modern living. She clarifies her stance when she remarks: "Serious writers these days don't write uplifting books because what they see around them is not uplifting" and avers, "but for me the novel is a social vehicle. It reflects society."[3] Although postmodern critic, Linda Hutcheon does not find *Life Before Man* a "straight forward realist novel,"[4] one has to take into account Atwood's observations, who categorically says that her novel "stays very firmly within the boundaries of realism." Critics are disappointed in it, however, because "it did not have the things in it that they were looking for," admits the author, and that is "why many people have missed its social and political content."[5] Hence, both in the form she employs and the content she expresses, Atwood attempts to highlight the sterility of the modern urban world. Nevertheless, the story does not stop with the presentation of social problems. It goes deeper and probes the psyche of three characters affected by their social and familial problems.

What transpires from the critics' views is that the characters go through the motions of everyday life and stick to their civilised routines. They resemble automations or fossils when they show a "boring sameness." But these critics fail to take into consideration the fact that these characters have their emotional needs, fears and difficulties. With the help of Horneyan tenets, we can understand their separate points of view, though all the three are occupied with identical problems of everyday life. Once we understand their value system, we would also comprehend the discrepancy between their outward behaviour and the world of their subjective feelings, and how they cope with the problems of life and death within the given milieu which is ordinary, routine and protean.

Elizabeth is a product of a home which does not have a congenial atmosphere. Her father was mostly absent and finally disappeared. Whenever he was at home he did nothing but played practical jokes on her mother and made her cry. Such a man who appears to his daughter a "turd", is incapable of giving her economic and emotional security. Elizabeth recalls: "She wasn't angry with her father. She'd always suspected he couldn't be depended on. She was angry with her mother for not having known it" (LBM, p. 152). This shows that her maternal connections also fill her with anger and shame and seem to reinforce her sense of low self-concept. Auntie Muriel's version is that her mother was no good, therefore, Elizabeth feels that she herself was probably no good. Thus, the role model fails to generate self-esteem in her. Moreover, her environment has nobody who could give her sympathy and affection, or take an interest in her needs.

Elizabeth's aunt is important in her life in a negative manner. She acts not only as a source of humiliation and deprivation but also to some extent as a model and reinforcer of certain tendencies. One scholar even points that "Elizabeth's blackout at her (Auntie Muriels's) grave seems... a subsequent rebirth of the woman."[6] It symbolically indicates that Muriel is reborn in Elizabeth. Paul Goetsch, attesting Hutcheon's contention says, "like Muriel in her life time, Elizabeth is going to raise two children 'single alone'..."[7] However, my purpose is not to go into the correctness of their contention but simply to point out that Auntie Muriel influenced Elizabeth. Atwood also confirms this when she tells Alan Twigg, "she had a bad childhood and she got locked into a struggle with her aunt" (*Conversations*, p. 125).

Observing Auntie Muriel's influence in Elizabeth, Nate remarks "the aunt had been important in Elizabeth's life. In his opinion the importance of something to someone had nothing to do with the positive qualities but only with its impact, its force, and the aunt had been a force" (LBM, p. 338). In case of Joan Delacourt in *Lady Oracle*, her aunt provided her freedom from the stifling atmosphere of her home and also economic security by leaving her money to carve out her own life and ultimately to accept the lived reality. On the contrary, Muriel did not provide freedom to Elizabeth. Instead, Elizabeth experiences a cramped in feeling, as if Auntie Muriel owns her. She pays her bills and "therefore, she owned her." This generated in her the feelings of insecurity. The self-righteousness of her aunt proves a destructive force in her healthy development. In the history of the arrogant-vindictive person, writes Horney, we usually find that the child has been forced to stifle his softer feelings and to undergo "a hardening process in order to survive" (NHG, p. 202). Elizabeth also suppresses the softer parts of her nature which leave her vulnerable or which interfere with her compensatory strategies. The fact that "Elizabeth had not wept or crawled," ((LBM, p. 152) shows how her emotional development had been impaired.

In terms of the Maslowian hierarchy, Elizabeth is frustrated in her needs for safety, love and belonging and self-esteem and is, therefore, arrested at an early stage of psychological development. It is evident in these remarks, "when she's with Auntie Muriel she is still part child. Part prisoner, part orphan, part cripple, part insane; Auntie Muriel the implacable wardress" (LBM, pp. 136-37). Childhood was not a period of fun for Elizabeth. In Elizabeth's own words "It's a revel, one of the many from which she once felt and still feels excluded." She recalls "they weren't allowed to dress up and shout in the streets like the others. They had to go to bed early and lie in the darkness, listening to the distant laughter" (LBM, pp. 38-39). These words remind us of Anita Desai's Bim in *Clear Light of the Day*,[8] for whom childhood had not been a happy period. She tells Tara that she would not like to return to her childhood. Traumatic experiences of childhood lead to various psychological problems. Charles Dickens's Esther in *Bleak House*, Charlotte Brontë's Jane in *Jane Eyre* always fly from decision-making and create problems for themselves just because their uncertain childhood did not let them develop the ability to decide. But the difference lies in their growth: Esther, Bim and Jane are self-effacing and withdrawn, whereas Elizabeth becomes aggressive. This shows the impact of culture. Esther and Jane belong to 19th century England, when morals for girls were strict, Bim is an Indian who is supposed to live within the cultural mores of the society. Not so for Elizabeth; she is a 20th century Canadian woman and she knows how to survive in a consumer society with its victim-victor syndrome. She develops a strong survival instinct and a "backbone of a rhinoceros." She herself admits "I have a very strong survival instinct. If you try to push me overboard, I'll take at least one of you down with me" (LBM, p. 175). And the omniscient narrator corroborates it: "If anyone pushed her, she pushed back twice as hard" (LBM, p. 166). This survival strategy is at the root of her conviction that she is invincible.

Aggressiveness, invincibility and the habit of seeing herself as a survivor of all odds, make her a narcissist. She believes that in any contest "she would win" (LBM, p. 166). These neurotic traits help her gain mastery in life. Narcissism is one of the subdivisions of the expansive solution. According to Horney, a narcissist believes that "he should be able to master the adversities of fate, the difficulties of the situation, the intricacies of intellectual problems, the resistance of other people, conflicts in himself" (NHG, p. 192). Elizabeth's basic solution is that of mastery of life. It chiefly entails her determination, conscious or unconscious, to overcome every obstacle in or outside herself. Her feeling of mastery lies in her firm belief that there is nothing she cannot do. There are no lines in her life, "these lines don't exist." She asserts further "she'll stop at nothing" (LBM, p. 168). For such a person, getting her way is not a difficult task. Moreover, in order to get what she wants she makes it a point to be charming and civilised, particularly when new people come into her orbit.

She idealises herself as a superior being, a "supermom" as Martha, a woman love of Nate, calls her. Elizabeth feels she is capable of fighting her way in life without being morbid like Nate or destructive like Chris. She knows "she will win, there's no way she can help winning. She'll win and she hopes it will make her feel better" (LBM, p. 305). She secretly embarks upon a search for glory in order to get the satisfaction of experiencing herself as her grandiose self. When she marries Nate against the advice of her aunt, she shows her strength to embark on her journey alone, despite her aunt. Her exuberance and vivacity following this action of independence strike a contrast to her sister and Nate. This gives her not only a vindictive triumph but also reinforces the sense of her uniqueness and independence. She exudes self-confidence: "She has backbone. She has money in the bank, not enough but some. She does not have to depend, she is not dependant. She is self-supporting" (LBM, p. 157). This gives her a semblance of a positive attitude. As she experiences herself as a superior being she tends to be expansive in her striving and belief about what she can achieve. She tends to be more or less openly arrogant, ambitious, demanding.

Karen Horney does not employ the term 'Narcissism' to mean an egocentric love of oneself. In Freudian literature, it means every kind of self-inflation, egocentricity, anxious concern with one's welfare and withdrawal from others. But to Horney, narcissism stands for a broad concept when one is "in love with one's idealized image" (LBM, p. 194). It is one of the several solutions of conflict between expansive and self-effacing drives. In her expansive solution Elizabeth also identifies herself with her glorified self. Like Peer Grant, she seems to say "I exist only as a superior being." She does not say it openly as Hagar does in Margaret Laurence's novel *The Stone Angel*, "there is no one like me in the world."[9] On the contrary, Elizabeth's behaviour and inner thinking substantiate what she thinks of herself. In *The Stone Angel*, while exploring the implication of the grandiose self, Laurence highlights the fact that pride in one's unique and false self-esteem deprives one of the gratifying relationship with one's fellow beings. In the long run, Hagar's pride leads her only to an emotional wilderness.

Coming back to *Life Before Man*, we find that in the beginning of the novel, Elizabeth's pride and self-esteem force her to condemn others. "Lesje is a clown," a curatorial assistant, and Martha a "garbage mouth". Thus, she displays her superiority in her relationship with others, in her behaviour, strivings and attitude towards life in general. In her social life especially in party games (Life Boat), she makes Lesje feel deficient and look small and uncultivated. Lesje, like Elinor in *Sense and Sensibility* or Anne Elliot in *Persuasion*, hides her humiliation and leaves the room quickly. At another occasion Elizabeth asks Martha, "Why not be friendly?... we might as well behave like reasonable adults" (LBM, p. 116). One scholar observes that in this display of manners "she is ironically enough successor to her Aunt Muriel." The puritanical spinster Muriel represents the ethical code of a bygone age, she (Elizabeth) "comes to stand for the 'enlightened' manners of the age of sexual liberation."[10] These strivings display her expansive drives and it becomes clear that she seeks sense of worth through recognition and mastery.

To gain mastery over life she can be generous, with a scintillating display of feelings, with flattery, with favours and help in anticipation of admiration or in return for devotion received. Other characters in the novel who come in contact with her, assess her according to their interaction. Martha calls Elizabeth "condescending and remote," to Lesje she is "goddamned discreet," while to Nate she is "very civilized" (LBM, p. 279). This condescending behaviour makes her worthy of notice of people which is reflected in these remarks: "There was always that unvoiced accusation, directed at her as if who she was, the way she spoke" (LBM, p. 61). Indeed, it satisfies her pride system to be the centre of attraction because it guarantees her uniqueness. It is her neurotic demand that she entertains Nate's women friends and endows them with glowing tributes. She praises Nate to them as a "sensational father" and remarks "you couldn't ask for a better one. The girls adore him" (LBM, p. 164). When it comes to showing discreet behaviour she does not hesitate to appreciate Lesje. She calls her a "congenial person." True to the attributes of a narcissist, she can be quite tolerant and does not expect others to be perfect. She adopts these measures to get the confirmation of her superior image in the form of admiration and devotion. That she succeeds in her efforts is substantiated by Lesje's remarks, that Elizabeth is a "queen out of a Shakespearean play" (LBM, p. 67), a woman with "competent maternal manners." To Marianne, she is "haute Wasp" (LBM, p. 106). Nate at the beginning of their love affair adores Elizabeth as "Madonna in a shrine" and "a second Florence Nightingale" (LBM, p. 50), very "understanding" and non-interfering. "She never tried to interfere with anything" (LBM, p. 30). These remarks show that she gets blind obedience from Nate and his friends. Hence, Elizabeth maintains her superior image. She gets these reinforcements from others to counterbalance her intrinsic demands with her grandiose self.

However, narcissist as she is, she is sure of herself and disdainful of others. She enjoys making a fool of them. "She'd known what she was doing. To be loved, to be hated, to be the centre" (LBM, p. 182). She is not bothered about others, "she knows what she looks like and she doesn't indulge in fantasies of looking any other way. She doesn't need her own reflection or the reflections of other people's ideas of her or of themselves" (LBM, p. 59). The manner of her gait also reflects her narcissism. She was "that dark point around which other colors swirl. She keeps her eyes straight, her shoulders level, her steps even. She marches" (LBM, p. 59). It will be correct to say that she marches on the path of self-glory and becomes her proud self. In her own words "I'm a mother... and I take that seriously. I would never leave an image like that behind for my children. I've had that done to me and I didn't like it" (LBM, pp. 107-108). She behaves in such a manner as long as these merely highlight her amiable and affable peculiarities and reinforce her grandiose self-image, but she must not be questioned seriously. When Martha attempts to probe her motives as to why she is generous instead of being envious of Nate's friends, she drops her. Being a narcissist she feels, rather, that her needs or tasks are so important that they entitle her to every privilege. She does not question her rights and expects others to love her unconditionally, no matter how much she actually trespasses on their rights. This is seen in her interpersonal relationship with Chris and Nate.

We have not explained why so independent and spirited a person like Elizabeth falls a prey to her passions, particularly for a man in Chris's position and what is that overwhelming force which attracts Elizabeth to Chris. Between Chris and Nate, we see that Nate too offers adoration and escape from the dreary existence of Auntie Muriel's place, as Chris does. He loves her devotedly as she had always longed to be loved but he can never satisfy, as Chris can, her need to submit and her desires for protection, power and conquest. Her "demon lover" fascinates her, she submits and is drawn to him because to see such a creature subdued by love for one would be a lot worth having.

One of the reasons why Elizabeth's love for Chris is so precious is that through it she can satisfy her own expansive drives. She enjoys her power over him. Chris admits to Elizabeth having power over him, "she had that power and she'd let him see it and touch it. She let him see he was deficient…" (LBM, p. 182). She cannot resist Chris's profession of devotion. Chris has brought to her a fantasy that attracts Elizabeth strongly. Secondly, Elizabeth's narcissist self needs to be the centre of attention and attraction. Chris and even his suicide fulfils that need.

Elizabeth enjoys her power over Chris and then drops him as if he had not been anything but "only a vacation" dream. The simplistic explanation she gives for her action is, "I treated him the way men treat women. A lot of men, a lot of women; but never me, not on your goddamned life. He couldn't take it" (LBM, p. 182). Feminist critics opine that Elizabeth's male-like treatment leads Chris in a reversal of roles to commit suicide and thus reiterate Chris as a female and Elizabeth as a male motif. To them, it appears that Atwood is examining the "power politics of intimate relations."[11] But the truth is that for Atwood, patriarchal structures of power and domination do not necessarily have a gender specific reference or relevance. As Frank Davey quite appropriately observes, "Atwood's male versus female dichotomy… is a metaphor rather than a literal distinction between men and women."[12] The "male" for Atwood becomes a metaphor for all dehumanising and despotic attitudinal and behavioural patterns that can as well issue from a woman as from a man. In *Life Before Man*, therefore, it is not Nate the man but Elizabeth the woman who, in her overpowering desire for a rule-bound and logocentric life, represents patriarchal power structures. According to these critics, in Atwood's value system, Elizabeth's belief in control and definition both for herself and others symbolise "male" attributes.

When interpreted from Horneyan tenets, they are not male attributes but the aggressive and expansive drives of the neurotic character. As already explained, because of her "bad childhood" she has become an expansive person. She has repressed her need for love and she expresses to fulfil her other needs which have been distorted. She wants power. The healthy drive for self-esteem is replaced by the self-idealisation and neurotic pride which generate the search for glory. The mastery of life to a narcissist like Elizabeth now lies in being independent. She wants to be in control of the situation. In her relationship with Chris she feels like the captive of love. She expresses the 'locked in' feelings thus:

> *Whenever I was with you I was in that room, even when we were outside, even when we were here. I'm in it now, only now you've locked the door… you don't want me ever to get out. You always knew I wanted to get out (LBM, pp. 20-21).*

Therefore, the predominant solution is to run away from such a relationship. Nothing can bind the narcissist, not even the love of a completely compliant person like Chris. No one can have power over her, not even Chris. When she finds Chris leaning on her, she hates him because he represents the claims of affection which she has ruthlessly excluded from her life. Nate does not have that kind of power, but Chris is trying to have, therefore, she drops him. Atwood, interpreting the title of *Life Before Man*, says that "for Elizabeth, it means that her own life is given priority over any relationship with a man."[13.] The Eliza-Chris affair is significant for Chris. Chris is a compliant person with low self-esteem and depends on Elizabeth for a sense of identity. He does not have the confidence to take charge of their life and its complicated affairs. He has the tendency to lean heavily on others, especially on Elizabeth, and expects her to solve all their psychic conflicts. Being a compliant person, it is natural for Chris to be drawn to an expansive person. He is drawn to Elizabeth not only because he needs to be protected by and to live vicariously through her who can master life aggressively, but also because he can only love someone who can "knock his own pride out from under him" (NHG, p. 245). She not only feeds his pride but breaks it too. No one else could master him as does Elizabeth.

Chris compulsively needs her love and subsequently her power. He is able to see the human possibility of power that would be within his reach with the magical help of Elizabeth. Her inner life gives him fresh insight. He admits that she made him realise what he wants to achieve in life. "She had what he wanted, power over a certain part of the world" (LBM, p. 182). When she wriggles out of his life, Chris reacts with a feeling of helplessness and impotence. Lesje understands towards the end of the novel why Chris committed suicide and she remarks: "it was this anger and the other thing, much worse, the fear of being nothing. People like Elizabeth could do that to you, blot you out" (LBM, p. 340). It is clear now that in an attempt to save himself from the assault of self-hate and feelings of nothingness, he commits suicide. Probably, it is an indirect manifestation of his power over her, even though Elizabeth walks out of his life.

Chris's suicide devastates Elizabeth and brings about the breakdown of her predominant solution. This denotes by implication, the impossibility of being and living her grandiose self. It also involves the responsibility of coming to terms with death. As Atwood remarks, "I had had a romantic, adolescent notion of death earlier, but I hadn't really felt that solid moment when you realize your life is not going to go on forever, that people you know aren't going to be here forever, that we're going to die."[14] With the suicide of Chris, Elizabeth reaches this solid moment, though it frightens her to confront the reality. She dreads the truth that people are not going to be there for ever, they die. She is alone. As Maslow points out, the truth carries with it the responsibility and that is an anxiety-producing state. The easiest way is to evade the consciousness of truth and to deny any feelings of guilt. Elizabeth reacts to Chris's suicide strongly. She hides her grief and denies any feelings of guilt. She oscillates between being responsible and not being guilty. She concedes, "I'm not sure whether or not I do feel guilty. I feel angry from time to time; otherwise I feel devoid. I feel as though I'm leaking electricity. I know I'm not responsible and that there's little I could have done and that he might have killed me or Nate or the children instead of himself" (LBM, p. 107).

Elizabeth displays outward poise and self-discipline after Chris's suicide, though she suffers horrible tumult within:

> *Yes I know I've suffered an unusual shock. I'm quite aware of that, I can feel the waves. I realize it was an act directed ostensibly at me though not really at me (LBM, p. 107).*

It disturbs her to think "that Chris's death was not something he did to himself... On the contrary as something he did to her... He's not feeling the effects of it, whereas she still is" (LBM, p. 151).

A healthy person would have expressed her grief openly and sought human sympathy from others. As a neurotic, Elizabeth is unable to do so. If she were to allow such feelings she would be flooded with self-contempt, she would violate the taboos of her expansive pride system and her compliant side would pass a very negative judgement on her aggressive behaviour. The hatred that she feels for compliant persons is in part a defense against and in part an externalisation of the self-hate which is generated by any emergence of the repressed yearnings. These self doubts and oscillations result in tension and anxiety. She feels lost, left out of events and is torn by conflicting shoulds. As she has come out as an impoverished person from childhood, her only way to solve her conflicts is to show that she cares for none and none can hurt her. Otherwise the realisation of unfulfilled shoulds elicits feelings of guilt and unworthiness. It is indispensable for her to use all available means to deny her failures to herself.

There are many occasions in the novel when she resorts to denial. When Chris's mother accuses Elizabeth of killing Chris, she resents this accusation. "No, she's said, more than once. It was malice, pride, it was his own damn fault. It wasn't me" (LBM, p. 181). This was her way of solving conflict: "Elizabeth doesn't care. She's practiced not caring" (LBM, p. 325). Under this hard exterior she is a feeling creature. Two contradictory emotions toss her: feeling powerful as well as threatened. Sometimes she feels the centre and feels that she has power. "Everything was fine as long as she was willing to pretend she was a cage, Nate a mouse, her heart pure cheese. He is, she knows, a hopeless sentimentalist. Earthmother, Nate her mole snouting in darkness while she rocked him" (LBM, p. 183). She also feels threatened, in case Nate were to move out. Therefore, there is something to be defended, something is to be done to persuade him to stay in.

She makes frantic efforts to fight the void in case Nate moves out. Her desperation is visible in her running to Lesje's apartment. She feels "They've locked her out. They're ignoring her, giggling in the bedroom while she stands down here in the night, discarded, invisible" (LBM, p. 291). This is indicative of her sufferings and conflict. She is filled with self-contempt; "anger, fury, denial." She is annoyed with herself for having allowed herself to be led to this ignominious, this vacant street. So preoccupied she is with Nate that she creates a web of fantasy around her.

In her fantasies, she visualises old age with Nate. This shows she needs love and companionship. "She wanted him to wind his arms around her, string on bone but warm bone, press her, comfort and rock her. She wanted to say: Can anything be saved? Meaning this wreck" (LBM, p. 110). She longs for his touch. "If Nate were with her, at least there would be something moving... I want to be moved. Move me" (LBM, pp. 109-10). But she also wants to eliminate all traces of self-effacing trends, all traces of self-doubt and self-contempt. As a refuge from her own nature and from the conflicts and imperfections of the human condition she again (after the suicide of Chris) takes up her search for glory and is ready to pay a heavy price for it.

Relationship with Nate after his moving out is instrumental in giving a renewed vision to Elizabeth. Elizabeth reorients herself. Her real self, eclipsed so far by her grandiose self, tries to emerge. It is presented symbolically. So far she has experienced herself as a grandiose person who is confident and in control of things. She sets rules which Nate follows. "It is the rule that when Elizabeth cooks, Nate does the dishes. One of the many rules, subrules, codicils, addenda, errata. Living with Elizabeth involves a maze of such legalities, no easier to understand because some of them are unspoken" (LBM, p. 184). She is not only in control of her life and Nate's life but also the love lives of Nate. She permits him the little diversions. She admits, "if she doesn't want a particular bone, anyone else is welcome to it" (LBM, p. 234). In fact, she supervises him as Martha says, "You wanted to supervise us. Like some kind of play ground organizer. Make sure it didn't go too far" (LBM, p. 165).

Any normal woman in her circumstances would have agreed to end this marriage which is marked by lack of communication and where "inter-personal fusion"[15] is missing. The importance of communication in human relationships is recognised by all authors. Here, I refer to an interview with Michel Fabre in which Margaret Laurence clearly states that to save human relationships from disintegration, people have to work hard at emotional communication. She says "I do not think that too many people actually do reach their potential in that way. I think that communications are difficult but we must keep on trying" (Michel Fabre, p. 68). "Between human individuals much of our deepest communication is at a non verbal level but at the same time... we can exchange emotions without words but we cannot exchange views. People can make love, people can hold and comfort their children, but in terms of exchanging our views of life and our responses to it we have to use words."[16] Elizabeth does not work at these communications. She does not worry about Nate's relationship with Lesje, but she minds his breaking away from her rules.

Though she does not love Nate any longer, she sticks to the marriage. R. D. Laing observes that some people are more disturbed by giving up a habitual game than by the loss of the partner. Elizabeth holds on to this marriage because her pride system and glorified image cannot tolerate breaking away from Nate. This would be her defeat. "She refuses to be deserted against her will. She refuses to be pathetic" (LBM, p. 236). If at all she agrees to break away from Nate, it has to be her decision. She would set the rules of Nate's freedom. This is in keeping with her neurotic pride and value system. She will have to tell him to go. "If she can't save anything else from the wreckage she will save face. They'll have a civilized discussion and they will both agree they are doing the best thing for the children. She will then be able to repeat this conversation to her friends, communicating her joy at this solution to all their problems, radiating quiet confidence and control" (LBM, p. 235). This would have restored her self-esteem and salvaged her neurotic pride.

With Nate's moving out without her consent, she is exposed to the failure of her expansive solution. The reality of the situation frightens her. She feels that she is manipulated and Nate has made a fool of her. Horney points out that a narcissist is extremely proud of fooling everybody and in his arrogance and contempt for others, believes that he actually succeeds in this. Conversely, he is most afraid of being fooled himself. Elizabeth, similarly, feels profound humiliation when she discovers that Nate has actually moved out. She resents "being taken a fool. Any ninny could have told he was packing; why did he bother to deny it? As for his moronic performance with the midnight fried liver and Harry Belafonte records, a two year old could see through it" (LBM, p. 235). She couldn't see through it and feels shattered by the fact that Nate could do this to her. "It's like being beaten at an intricate and subtle game of chess by the world tiddlywinks champion" (LBM, p. 236). She feels lonely and devastated.

Loneliness forces her to live through the traumatic experiences of her life again – the death of her mother, a drinker by fire, the suicide of her sister Caroline in the bathtub of an asylum, the strict puritanic education and finally her aunt's death. While taking a bath, she toys with the idea of committing suicide but she decides against it. "I know I have to keep on living and I have no intention of doing otherwise" (LBM, p. 107). She counters her dilemma by finding within her an ability to survive, not to go on living but to change and to move into new areas of life. Though she makes a regressive choice after Nate's moving and goes with William and goes with the salesman, she saves herself from harm. She struggles to survive and commits herself to life. She sees the stark reality that life is a routine, it has to be lived, you cannot escape it. Gradually she learns to accept both her past and future as she says, "I am an adult and I do not think I am merely the sum of my past. I can make choices and I suffer the consequences, though they aren't always the ones I foresaw" (LBM, p. 108). Such elevating thoughts help her in seeing life in its proper perspective.

Auntie Muriel's revelation in the hospital alters Elizabeth's perception. She used to see her aunt as a tyrannical figure. "She has always hated her and she always will hate her, she will not forgive her. This is an old vow, an axiom" (LBM, p. 327). But, her newly gained perception helps her to accept Auntie Muriel as "her own burning mother" (LBM, p. 328). She ritualistically "takes Auntie Muriel's blinded hands... soothing them with her thumbs as in illness she has soothed the hands of her children" (LBM, p. 328) and forgets all about her vow and herself. It will not be out of place here to compare these feelings of Elizabeth to that of Hagar's feelings of compassion in *The Stone Angel*. Hagar does not die as a pessimist and alienated individual. From her experience of complete isolation, at last, Hagar experiences one epiphanic moment of life. She sheds all her ideas of self when she meets the insurance salesman Murray Lees; they cry together over the children they have lost. Hagar's feelings are awakened, she is able to feel compassion and to do two good acts at the age of ninety. First, she lies to her son Marvin telling him that he is a better son to her than John and secondly, she fetches the bedpan for Sandra Nong. This experience enables her to perceive an affirmative vision of life. She asks the priest to sing to the Lord with joyful voice. "He sang for me and it did me good," says Hagar.

Her altered perception also did good to Elizabeth. Atwood admits that this human support which Elizabeth gives to her aunt is something positive and sees in this a possibility of Elizabeth's change. She thinks she will come out of herself:

> *When she is finally able, not exactly to forgive her aunt, but at least to go through the motions of giving human support, that's positive. Even though she doesn't feel compassion, she acts it out anyway. After that happens, there's a chance she will be able to get outside herself... By the end of the book there's a possibility of change. I never make Prince charming endings because I don't believe in them. But I do believe that people can change. May be not completely but some.*[17]

Elizabeth's creator is right. Elizabeth relates herself to people in their sufferings. She sees the actuality of life and struggles and commits herself to life. She accepts the dissolution of her marriage, loses her husband to a younger woman and faces the problem of age. She accepts Nate's independence only when the burden of the past seems to be lifted from her after the burial of Muriel. She frees Nate and feels relieved that "war is over, discussed." In freeing Nate, she also experiences her own "freedom from that set of rules" against which she was measured always by him and "his pious nun faced mother", "she will be free of that... but she thinks she can live that" (LBM, p. 238). She experiences freedom; freedom without a sense of responsibility is incomplete, a pure licence. She feels responsible for her children, she will raise them "single" and "alone". Now in the actual sense of the term she has survived, she has survived Chris's death and Nate's moving out. In order to attain that freedom, she has tossed between the pressures of neurotic needs and her affirmative will to live with the children alone. Her journey to and fro indicates her self-doubts. Now with Nate's moving out and Muriel's death, Elizabeth grapples with her authentic self. Between Lesje's outbursts and Nate's withdrawal, Elizabeth stands as an emerging self.

Lesje is a young palaeontologist who is caught in the web of what Martin Buber calls "self-contradictions." She is not aware of the alienation caused by the desire of the self to recoil or escape from the contingencies of life. She oscillates between contradictory forces: withdrawal and involvement, detachment and attachment, the need to withdraw in order to preserve one's wholeness and sanity and the need to be involved in the painful process of life. She takes recourse to fantasising as an alternative to her conflicts. It is important to compare her to Joan Foster in *Lady Oracle*. Both are fantasisers but for Joan, it would mean "there was no fantasy and therefore no escape" (LO, p, 270). Lesje has a similar regressive need to escape from the boring and threatening present to a prehistoric world of her own making. She dreams of a better life "before man" among the dinosaurs of the Mesozoic period. Her "restful fantasy" of the Mesozoic world is the imaginative violation of the "official version of palaeontological reality." It is safe compared to the life outside, especially for the "insecure and tentative Lesje". To cope with the outside world, she lacks Elizabeth's "socialized power and control" and turns to this cataloguing work and her science-inspired fantasies to create a work she can control. One scholar remarks that Lesje turns to the (learned but childlike) fantasy world, "both to compensate for, and to offer escape from life... (This) world that is left behind at the end of the novel as life and creativity – in the form of her unborn child – assert themselves."[18] Margaret Atwood also makes it clear that fantasy provides Lesje a means to escape the dreary present.

Psychologists agree that daydreams and fantasies are important for the human psyche; they represent wish fulfilment and stand for symbolic satisfaction. It was Freud who first pointed out links in motivation between creative imagination and daydreams. In Lesje's life, the relevance of fantasy is also from a different angle. She escapes temporarily from the despair of abject life. It soothes her; she "finds it restful", "it stops that small noise in her mind, the worrying of something trapped behind the woodwork" (LBM, p. 241). These remarks do give a semblance of peace but when seen from the Horneyan angle, she is making a move to withdraw from life and its complications. She runs to the world of dinosaurs and fantasises if they come to life. Dinosaurs "aren't a religion for her only a preserve." They serve as a haven, a refuge for her. She admits that "All she wants is a miracle, because anything else is hopeless" (LBM, p. 314). Some of Atwood's heroines run from their dual or fragmented identity while others like Elaine in *Cat's Eye* and Joan Foster in *Lady Oracle* run from their multiple identities. Lesje runs to this Mesozoic world because of the loss of her identity.

This daydreaming is interpreted differently by different scholars. For Paul Goetsch, Lesje's daydreams show human beings as clumsy as dinosaurs. They have "difficulties in communicating with each other and regulating their relations, and, like some types of dinosaurs, they have special problems in connection with love and sexuality. In Lesje's regressive fantasies, the dinosaurs sometimes represent life before humans, but in other daydreams of the young woman they also stand for passion or for extinction." [19] From these daydreams, it becomes clear that Lesje relates herself to dinosaurs. She finds it difficult to communicate with people, "She was much happier among concrete things" (LBM, p. 66). She is showing a pattern of alienation of the severest kind, leading to her neurosis. Withdrawal as an escape from the complexities of life is not a health-inducing device. It does not lead to self-communion but alienation from the self. This alienation is working in her interpersonal relationship as well as on her psyche. The sterility of her relationship with William is reflected in their frequent conversations about the end of life. She speaks of the extinction of dinosaurs and William, an environment engineer, talks about the destruction of nature and mankind. She is alienated from real life. She can neither respond to nor understand love between man and woman:

> *Lesje isn't sure what she means by 'in love'. Once she thought she was in love with William, since it upset her that he did not ask her to marry him... At first she welcomed the relative simplicity, even the bareness, of their life together. They were both committed to their jobs, and they had, it seemed, easily met expectations and only minor areas of friction. But Nate has changed things, he has changed William. What was once a wholesome absence of complications is now an embarrassing lack of complexity (LBM, p. 140).*

Only an alienated person can make remarks about love like that. In the words of Erich Fromm, love is "an interpersonal fusion". For Lesje and William, it is avoiding the responsibility, "Each wanted the other to take the responsibility" (LBM, p. 23). William's absence does not disturb Lesje and she finds it difficult to dream of William. In her opinion, it is a "sign of maturity that his absences don't disturb her..." These are not signs of maturity as Lesje claims but signs of alienation. This live-in-relation with William is need-based and we can easily call it workable adjustment. It is not love as Lesje sometimes wants to believe, it is a mutual admiration which has no commitment. "He admires her mind... He tells her she has beautiful hair. He gazes into her sloe eyes. He's proud of her as a trophy and as a testimony to his own wide-mindedness" (LBM, p. 26). She admires him, she likes his "optimism, his belief that every catastrophe is merely a problem looking for a brilliant solution" (LBM, p. 24). Their love comes to this: they admire each other and "they live together". Horneyan tenets say that a neurotic with withdrawal tendencies cannot go for a deeper relationship. Lesje's feelings for William show no depth. She herself admits that the loss of William is a breach of trust, not much cause for mourning. It simply hurts. "The loss of William, familiar William, does hurt after all. Not because of William himself, but because she trusted him simply, uncaring and unthinking. She trusted him like a sidewalk, she trusted him to be what he seemed to be, and she will never be able to do that with anyone again. It isn't the violence but the betrayal of this innocent surface that is so painful; though possibly there was no innocence, possibly she made it up" (LBM, p. 225). It is familiarity not intimacy that characterises their relationship. The relationship with William is a matter of routine for her. "She realizes now that her life with William... [is] daily routine. Routines hold you in place. Without them she floats weightless" (LBM, p. 242). Lesje recalls the times when her affair with William was simple-minded and joyously adolescent.

Loss of a friend or lover would move any young girl of her age. But she has never felt as a teenager when she was one herself. She narrates an incident of her high school days when the teacher asked them to read *Romeo and Juliet*, thinking it would appeal to them because it was about teenagers. Lesje confesses that she "hadn't felt like a teenager" (LBM, p. 224), instead she filled the margins of the work with drawings of ferns. There are many other instances of this alienation. She recalls another incident: in Grade Five, she had been asked to write about "My Summer Holiday". She was supposed to write about something personal, something from her own life. Instead she wrote about rock-collection. That was something personal from her life. This impersonal attitude remains with her even as an adult. She has no "close friends" and after losing William, she is alone. But this loss and absence is not soul deep because as an alienated person, she is incapable of experiencing pain and loss.

Lesje's psychological alienation can be ascribed to her unfortunate home which leaves the child insecure and isolated. In this connection, it is relevant to mention the nurturing role of the mother. Lesje's mother could not provide proper nurturing to the child Lesje. She was a working woman and before Lesje was old enough to go to school, she left her [Lesje] under the care of her two grandmothers (paternal and maternal), half the week with each. Her grandmother Etlin was Jewish while Grandmother Symlski was Ukrainian. If the grandmothers were loving and had shown consistency and care, Lesje would have grown into a healthy person. But they fought and showed anger at each other. If one would give Lesje decorated eggs to play with, the other would smash them with her boots. As Lesje recalls they "fought over her as if she's been a dress at bargain." They "had focused their rage... on each other. As for her, they'd both loved her, she supposes; and both had mourned over her as if she were in some way dead. It was her damaged gene pool. Impure, impure" (LBM, p. 69). This hostile environment threatened her and developed in her a sense of insecurity and filled her with anxiety. The result is that Lesje could not develop a distinctive identity.

In addition to the hostile environment at home, her multi-cultural and racial background also damaged her sense of identity. She does not feel either purely Jewish or Ukrainian. When she was nine, one of her aunts explained to her, "Lesje isn't really Jewish. She could be classified as truly Jewish only if it was her mother" (LBM, p. 98). Lesje finds her Ukrainian name intriguing, "though a little funny". As Joan's borrowed name from the silver screen problematised her sense of identity in *Lady Oracle*, Lesje's Ukrainian name created problems for her (Lesje). In either group, "she was an outsider looking in. She felt as excluded as if she'd been surrounded by a crowd of her own cousins. On both sides. Kiss me, I'm multicultural" (LBM, p. 101). At the beginning of the novel, she feels that because of her multicultural background, William and his family do not fully acknowledge her as an individual. Even in her relation with Nate, she feels she is dismembered: she does not belong to any group. "There is already a group of Mrs Schoenhofs: one is Nate's mother, the other is the mother of his children. Lesje isn't the mother of anyone; officially she is nothing" (LBM, p. 310). She has no identity, "she is only a pattern," which will "dissolve" someday (LBM, pp. 191-192). This psychic condition of alienated Lesje reminds us of George Lamming's description of the natives. George Lamming, the Caribbean writer, in his work *The Pleasures of Exile* describes the West Indian or the Native as "exiled from his gods, exiled from his nature, exiled from his name." Lesje is also exiled. She has no moorings in this alien world.

If the world is alien and hostile, the easiest course is to withdraw from it. Lesje adopts the strategies of withdrawal and compliance, alternately. She is caught up between the conflicting ambitions of warring grandmothers and her parents. She remembers how her Ukrainian grandmother had wanted her to be an airline stewardess while her Jewish grandmother had wanted her to be a lawyer and also to marry another lawyer if possible. "Her father wanted her to make the most of herself. Her mother wanted her to be happy" (LBM, p. 126). Every human being has a self which includes an awareness of being human, individual and capable of making choices that affects one's life and that of others. The choice of Lesje is limited in this environment. To "stay out of the way" (LBM, p. 70) is her primary strategy to solve her conflicts. There is no move on her part, to participate in living, to strive for achievement, to socialise.

Her parents sensed her unsociability and realised that she was becoming too wrapped up in a world of her own. In order to make her "more sociable," they gave her dancing lessons but as the narrator puts it, it was "too late". She could not be sociable. For this, they blamed silently, of course, her grandmother Etlin. This delineates the psychic turmoil, fear and anxiety of Lesje who fails to relate to her world. Rollo May has an explanation for cases such as these. Lesje has lost, what May terms "intentionality." Intentionality gives a person orientation or direction:

> *By intentionality, I mean the structure which gives meaning to experience... Intentionality is at the heart of consciousness. I believe that it is also the key to the problem of wish and will... It is the structure of meaning which makes it possible for us, subjects that we are, to see and understand the outside world, objective as it is. In intentionality, the dichotomy between subject and object is partially overcome.*[20]

In the case of Lesje, her false self sees herself as an independent person, above all socialisation and competition. She likes to imagine herself "watching through binoculars, blissful, uninvolved." This is the demand of her idealised self. To save herself from self-berating, she quickly builds around her a citadel of self-glorifying virtues commensurate with her withdrawn self. She knows, "she's regressing." She is also aware that "she's been doing that a lot lately. This is a daydream left over from her childhood and early adolescence, shelved sometime ago in favour of other speculations. Men replaced dinosaurs, true, in her head as in geological time; but thinking about men has become too unrewarding. Anyway, that part of her life is settled for the time being" (LBM, p. 13). Nothing is settled, though her idealised self wants to believe it.

In reality, she is experiencing a conflict between compliant and resigned drives. These tendencies pull her in opposite directions. She must keep a safe emotional distance yet she cannot help being drawn to Nate. Her attitude of resignation warns her that she must avoid any entanglement. These observations work on her unconscious, the wish to win Nate's love figures there. Consciously or unconsciously her efforts have been to get a positive response from her family. Insecure as she is, she is usually afraid of saying the wrong thing anyway and likes to play the role of the appeaser. "She's an appeaser and she knows it" (LBM, p. 65). As an ideal daughter, she devotes her efforts to appease her mother. "Lesje's mother... wants her to appear to be happy. Lesje's happiness is her mother's justification. Lesje has known this forever and is well practiced at appearing, if not happy, at least stolidly content..." (LBM, p. 225). In Horneyan terminology, it is the trait of the self-effacing person. Persons belonging to this category place curbs "on all that is presumptuous, selfish and aggressive" (NHG, p. 219). Lesje also cripples her capacity to fight, to demand her rights, to be self-assertive. Her life pattern amply illustrates it. She is appeasing her mother and attending to William's needs and her self-denial goes so far that she does not like to speak about herself and wishes to become the woman Nate believes she is.

In doing so she is pushing her resigned tendencies to the background. One encounters a withdrawn and uninvolved Lesje so often in the novel that one finds it hard to believe that Lesje is basically a self-effacing woman. But, if we read closely, we realise that the need to become Nate's version indicates her unconscious longing to be loved. She wears around herself a fantasy world. She fantasises about him and also about her life. She expects some sudden and unaccountable change, as if "something momentous is about to take place. Her life is about to change: things will not be as they have been before" (LBM, p. 140). True to the traits of a compliant character, she wants to become Nate's image and is sure that love can change her life. For Nate, Lesje is another 'romance icon,' the unattainable, other-worldly "exotic". "Holding Lesje," Nate muses, "would be like holding some strange plant, smooth, thin, with sudden orange flowers. Exotics, the florists called them" (LBM, p. 76). Both are victims of each others' fantasy. He expects her to be serene, "a refuge; he expects her to be kind. He really thinks she is, underneath... He ought to be able to tell by now that she isn't like this at all. Nevertheless she wants to be; she wants to be this beautiful phantom, this boneless wraith he's conjured up. Sometimes she really does want it" (LBM, p. 310). He manages to convey to Lesje that he "respects her, admires her and desires her" and that he does not want, just an affair with her. He wants to have a child by her. These remarks reinforce her self-image and raise her self-esteem. She feels the barometer of self-worth rising.

Loving Nate can be interpreted as an act of goodness. Lesje is able to rationalise many of her guilt feelings and to bring her acts into mental accord with her self-effacing value system. She seizes upon Nate's unhappiness and his need of her to justify her seeing him. On his part, he doesn't want her to "think she's breaking up a marriage" (LBM, p. 141). These statements of Nate give her a solid ground for rationalisation. "She doesn't feel like another woman; she isn't wheedling or devious, she doesn't wear negligees or paint her toe-nails. William may think she's exotic, but she's not really; She's straightforward, narrow and unadorned, a scientist; not a web-spinner, expert at the entrapment of husbands" (LBM, pp. 141-142). Such thoughts lift her up and she tells herself that she is not involved in some conventional triangle but is following an honourable affair.

She believes that she is living her ideal image. She rationalises that Nate's family is "surely external to him; in himself he's single, a free agent. And Elizabeth is therefore not the wife of Nate, she isn't a wife at all instead she's widow, Chris's widow, if anyone's" (LBM, p. 142). She lives under these pretences that Nate may be the father of her children but he is not Elizabeth's husband. Her argument is: "They haven't lived together, he means slept together for several years, he isn't sure how many. They've stayed in the same house together because of the children" (LBM, p. 141). Her self-esteem rises and falls with the attention and inattention she receives. Sometimes she feels very important because Nate loves her. Sometimes she feels exiled from his life. A vacuum forms around her heart, spreads; it is as if she doesn't exist. Nate's absences irk her. "In the absence of Nate, who has offered, when she comes to think of it, nothing at all. A wide plain. A risk" (LBM, p. 162). She is swayed by the feelings of being nothing, "cipher", "superfluous". Self-hate overpowers her. She feels that her relationship with Nate is a blunder, "she's blundered into something tangled and complex, tenuous, hopelessly snarled" (LBM, p. 240). She feels condemned in her relations to Nate's children. She bursts with a sense of wrongs and self-hate. "I want to feel I'm living with you," she said. "Not with you and your wife and children" (LBM, p. 278). She cannot do anything to change this situation and self-contempt grips her.

Having sex in Elizabeth's bed gives a devastating blow to her ideal image. She feels she has wronged Elizabeth. Guilt sweeps her balance off. "This is horrible, this is a violation. She feels grubby; it's almost like an incest" (LBM, pp. 190-91). Till now she has been successful in warding off guilt which came by being another woman. Her self-image crumbles like a piece of cardboard. It hurts her to think that "she and Elizabeth are interchangeable. Or his feeling that Elizabeth's bed is still in some sense his also, he can do whatever he wants in it" (LBM, p. 191). These are the moments when she feels a "mean minded ogre". Hatred and loneliness, which she had kept under check, also surface with intensity and she feels lost and condemned, "isolated, single, childless and culpably young, she was made to stand in penance, watching a pantomime she could not decipher" (LBM, p. 259). Lesje is not only helpless in the face of her circumstances but also rendered weak and unassuming by her self-effacing drives.

Lesje finds a release through an unhysterical change in perspective when she temporarily identifies herself with Chris and then throws away the contraceptive pills. She gives up her passivity and decides to opt for life. "If children were the key, if having them was the only way she could stop being invisible, then she would goddamn well have some herself" (LBM, p. 341). Her decision to stop using the pills and bear Nate's child is symbolic of her new found will to act and signals her altered self-perspective and a new beginning. Lesje discovers her power to act positively for herself and not to commit suicide that would negate the fundamental strength of her nature. Thus, Lesje moves from passive acceptance to active participation. Atwood views Lesje's pregnancy as "one of those profoundly meaningful human activities which can be very multifaceted and resonant. It can have a very positive meaning for some people and a very negative meaning for others" (Conversations, p. 142). She does not agree with those who assert that pregnancy fulfils Lesje's femininity, nor does she corroborate that it is anti-feminist to get pregnant. She defines her feminism "as human equality and freedom of choice."[21] Stouck views in this decision an offering of hope. He remarks: "This instinct to continue the species, to defy mortality, may have no rational basis... Yet the fact of survival and another generation is an offering of hope."[22] There is definitely a hope in Lesje's life. She gives up the evasion offered by the fantasy world and relates herself to life.

It will not be out of place here to compare Lesje's decision to have a child with that of the narrator's decision in *Heat and Dust* which, according to a critic, is tension reducing. Discussing the narrator-protagonist's decision in *Heat and Dust*, the scholar observes that "in her decision to be a mother there lies the question of free choice which is existential in itself."[23] Morag's decision to bear Jules' child in *The Diviners*[24] also reflects her need for relatedness not only in loving Jules but also in bearing his child, Pique. Pique becomes the link with the past she has so long denied and becomes the "harbinger of death, continuer of life" (p. 239). Similarly, in the case of Lesje, as Paul Goetsch comments, "the guardian of the past (p. 308) develops into the guardian of the future and joins the many mothers and mother figures of the novel."[25] She relates to other mothers like Elizabeth; she visualises the future when they would turn "... grandmothers". She realises that the "tension between the two of them is a difficulty for the children. They ought to stop" (LBM, p. 359). She does not see Elizabeth permanent like an icon, but "shorter, worn, ordinary;

mortal" (LBM, p. 359). This new way of viewing things makes her feel free. Becoming a mother gives her a fair measure of self-recognition. She regains her identity like Rachel Cameron does in Laurence's *A Jest of God*.[26] Lesje also nourishes the notion that the mere biological fact of having a child means that a woman has control of her life. This equips her to cope with the contingent reality.

The change of perception is felt in her attitudinal change towards her fantasy world. "The Mesozoic isn't real. It's only a word for a place you can't go to anymore because it isn't there" (LBM, p. 267). It has been her theoretical opinion that man is "a danger to the universe, a mischievous ape, spiteful, destructive, malevolent." Now she knows this is not true. She struggles to survive and commits herself to life. Even Virginia Woolf, who did not like to have her own children, admits that she can appear successful to herself only if she has children and she connects her failure to write well with having no children. Virginia Woolf gives her famous prescription for a woman writer in *A Writer's Diary*, "I don't like the physicalness of having children of one's own... I can dramatise myself a parent, it is true. And perhaps I have killed the feeling instinctively"; yet in another entry, she anguishes, "I want to appear a success even to myself, yet I don't... It's having no children... [that accounts for her] failing to write well."[27] Lesje is a "success" to herself.

From the patriarchal perspective one would expect the single woman [like Lesje] to be a figure of derision and social ostracism but as Annis Pratt says, "In much of women's fiction she becomes a hero representing the possibility of growth and survival."[28] Lesje has become a hero in this sense; she has shown growth as well as survival. The word "Survival" is defined differently by Margaret Laurence. She defines it as the "ability to continue experiencing relationship with others, to continue reaching out and giving and returning love."[29] Lesje has moved to active participation in life, "she has learned more than she ever intended to, more than she wants" (LBM, p. 343). She has always evaded the reality of the lived present but now the acceptance of her decision and the responsibility that follows that decision changes her life.

Both Lesje and Elizabeth, by owning responsibility, affirm life; in her next novel *Bodily Harm*, Atwood adopts a broader vision and lets Rennie Wilford reach affirmation by relating herself to her fellow human being. How Rennie, an alienated character, struggles under conflicts and finally grapples with reality, will be explored in the next chapter.

References

1. David Stouck, *Major Canadian Authors* (Lincoln and London: University of Nebraska Press, 1988), p. 287.

2. Sherill Grace, *Violent Duality*, p. 135.

3. Alan Twigg, "Just Looking at Things That Are There," in *Margaret Atwood: Conversations*, ed. Earl G. Ingersoll (Ontario: Ontario Review Press, 1990), p. 126.

4. Linda Hutcheon, *The Canadian Postmodern: A Study of Contemporary English-Canadian Fiction* (Toronto: Oxford University Press, 1988), p. 152.

5. Alan Twigg, p. 127.

6. Linda Hutcheon, "From Poetic to Narrative Structures: The Novels of Margaret Atwood," in *Margaret Atwood: Language, Text, And System*, ed. Sherrill E. Grace and Lorraine Weir (Vancouver: University of British Columbia Press, 1983), p. 24.

7. Paul Goetsch, "Margaret Atwood's, *Life Before Man* as a Novel of Manners," in *Gaining Ground*: European Critics on Canadian Literature, ed. Robert Kroetsch (Edmonton: Newest Press, 1985), pp. 144-45.

8. Anita Desai, *Clear Light of the Day* (New Delhi: Allied, 1980).

9. Margaret Laurence, *The Stone Angel* (Toronto: Seal Books, 1984), p. 223.

10. Paul Goetsch, "Margaret Atwood's *Life Before Man* as a Novel of Manners," in *Gaining Ground*, p. 139.

11. Annette Kolodny, "Margaret Atwood and The Politics of Narrative," p. 97.

12. Frank Davey, *Reading Canadian Reading* (Winnipeg: Manitoba Canada Turnstone Press, 1988), p. 90.

13. Alan Twigg, p. 123.

14. Alan Twigg, p. 126.

15. Erich Fromm, *The Art of Loving* (London: Harper Collin Publishers, 1957), p. 22.

16. Michel Fabre, "From *The Stone Angel* to *The Diviners*: An Interview with Margaret Laurence," in *A Place to Stand on*, p. 68.

17. Alan Twigg, *Margaret Atwood: Conversations*, p. 125.

18. Linda Hutcheon, *The Canadian Postmodern* (Toronto: Oxford University Press, 1988), p. 148.

19. Paul Goetsch, "Margaret Atwood's *Life Before Man* as a Novel of Manners," in *Gaining Ground*, p. 148.

20. Rollo May, *Love and Will* (New York: Norton, 1969), pp. 223-24.

21. Alan Twigg, *Margaret Atwood: Conversations*, p. 142.

22. David Stouck, *Major Canadian Authors*, p. 288.

23. Usha Bande, "Female Quest in *Heat and Dust*," in Iqbal Kaur ed. *Gender and Literature* (New Delhi: B. R. Publishing Corpn, 1992), p. 191.

24. Margaret Laurence, *The Diviners* (Toronto: McClelland and Stewart, 1974), p. 220.

25. Paul Goetsch, *Gaining Ground*, p. 146.

26. Margaret Laurence, *A Jest of God* (Toronto: McClelland and Stewart, 1966), p. 184.

27. Virginia Woolf, *A Writer's Diary*, ed. Leonard Woolf (1953; rpt. New York: New American Library, 1968), p. 29.

28. Annis Pratt, *Architypal Patterns in W's fiction* (Great Britain: The Harvester Press, 1982), p. 127.

29. Michel Fabre, "From *The Stone Angel* to *The Diviners*: An interview with Margaret Laurence," *A Place to Stand on*, ed George Woodcock (Edmonton Alberta: Newest Press, 1987), p. 65.

CHAPTER 6

Bodily Harm

*B*odily Harm is the story of Rennie Wilford, a Toronto-based journalist who visits two tiny Caribbean islands ostensibly to write a travel piece for her magazine *Visor* and to recover from a partial mastectomy. But, in reality, she is escaping from the ordinariness and humiliation of everyday living, as she is afraid of the approaching death with which mastectomy threatens her. Ironically, her escape to those islands involves her in bewildering events. After one point, her story reads like detective fiction with real murders, rapes, tortures, political intrigues, corruption, CIA agents and the smuggling of contraband goods which land her ultimately in prison as an assumed spy. This turn of events evoked different responses and reactions from scholars and critics. One scholar points out that after *Life Before Man*, Atwood is looking "at the abuse of power in the public arena".[1] According to B. W. Powe, in *Bodily Harm*, Atwood 'discovers' political commitment, which, however, is countered by Linda Hutcheon who feels that the novel is "about human rights and politics".[2] The author also asserts that she was "writing a spy story from the point of view of one of the ignorant peripherally involved women."[3]

That Rennie feels "peripheral" (BH, p. 226) is substantiated by her writings. She writes articles on life and superficial columns for magazines and newspapers and is content to lead an equally superficial and inconsequential life. She avoids what is in "bad taste" (26-27) or "out of date" in her professional life and remains an "expert on surfaces". In her interpersonal relationships, she denies herself the need to belong, because it made "you visible: soft, penetrable"; it made "you ludicruous":

> *It was foolhardy, and if you got through it without damage, it was only by sheer luck. It was like taking off your clothes at*

lunchtime in a bank. It let people think they knew something about you that you didn't know about them, it gave them power over you (BH, p. 102).

All she wants is a relationship without "strings, no commitment". But she liked Jake because he satisfied her need to be admired. It was a relief to have a man say "that he thought she had a terrific [body]" (BH, p. 104). It is her neurotic need to lose herself that makes her merge first with Jake, then with Daniel, in clinging relationships.

To satisfy her basic needs she clings to her grandmother in childhood. Her holding on to the edge of her grandmother's gown is symbolically her hold on "safety;" if "I let go I'll fall" (BH, p. 53). She seeks the same safety in her relationship with Jake or Daniel. They are her "magic helpers". Erich Fromm first used the term "magic helpers" and Horney acknowledges it. The term represents the outside power on whom a helpless or dependent person projects all his longings and develops a symbiotic relationship. For a morbidly dependent person, this relationship is his necessity. As Horney points out, "Assuming that she does manage to struggle out of her involvement by hook or crook... get out of one dependency only sooner or later to rush into another one" (NHG, p. 257). We get Horney's version of this relationship in *Self Analysis* and Fromm's in *Escape from Freedom*.

Rennie fits in the description of such dependent persons who crave for such magic helpers. Dependents as they are, they want someone to "protect, help, and develop" them and be with them constantly.[4] People are bound to magic helpers because of "an inability to stand alone". Having no faith in her own efforts, Rennie hopes to satisfy all her wishes through the magic helper. Her object is not to live her own life but to manipulate her partner and make him responsible for her well-being. Their dependency "results in a feeling of weakness and bondage" and a resentment that must be suppressed because it "threatens the security sought for in the relationship." Love of Jake makes Rennie feel not only secure but invulnerable too. She feels protected: when "she loved Jake, she loved everything. She felt she was walking inside a charmed circle: nothing could touch her, nothing could touch them" (BH, p. 72). It is a clear confirmation of the fact that she is living with her idealised image. She feels different, "she was unique" (BH, p. 22) but she is saved from that fate. Her mainstay in life is Jake whom she glorifies not only in her private life but also in public. She writes an article on him in *Visor* and derives vicarious strength. In this way she surrenders to Jake.

Horney's remark "love surrender appears as a solution for everything and hence as a vital necessity" (NHG, p. 246) is quite appropriate in Rennie's case. Her need for total surrender also makes it necessary for her to idealise the partner because she finds her unity only with Jake, to whom she can delegate her pride: "he should be the proud one and she the subdued," says Horney. "Both her need to idealize him and her need to surrender operate hand in hand" (NHG, p. 252). True to these traits of a compliant character, Rennie idealises Jake. He is "good at what he did," attractive and successful as a small company owner at the age of thirty. Her ability to attract such a person gives her a sense of great power and worth. That she is "passionately and voraciously desired" (BH, p. 101) lifts her image. She lives this idealised image, feeling "unique" (BH, p. 23) as a "good travel writer", happy that "there's nothing to worry about", and that "nothing can touch her... She's exempt" (BH, p. 203). She gets reinforcement of her image from her friends. All those with whom she interacts find her "nice", "sweet" and open. Whatever expansive traits she has, remains suppressed in her unconscious because consciously she does not want to be anything that nice. Paul's remarks are revealing when he chides her, "you're nice, you can't help it. Naive. But you think you have to prove you're not merely nice, so you get into things you shouldn't. You want to know more than other people, am I right?" (BH, p. 150). In Horneyan language, making a self-image and living it is tantamount to the Faustian "devil's pact." Rennie is living in the self-constructed world of complacency.

Two significant events break Rennie's smooth "surfaces": first, a house break by a supposedly male burglar with the possible implied threat to her life symbolised by the length of the rope he had left behind "coiled neatly on the quilt" (BH, p. 13) inspires fears because it dawns on her that she is not "exempt". She is ordinary and vulnerable. And second, the reality of an operation which shakes her and gives a glimpse of her irreparable shaken sensibility. "My life is the pits right now", she feels "she can't bear not knowing. She doesn't want to know" (BH, p. 60) the final diagnosis. Her contradictory reactions to knowing the doctor's diagnosis reveal her mental state. "She believed two things at once: that there was nothing wrong with her and that she was doomed anyway" (BH, p. 23). Her imagination takes full charge of her reasoning. She sees death lurking somewhere nearby. It is personified by the presence of a faceless stranger with a coiled rope in the room. Thus the theft is linked in her imagination with that of the impending doom. Her vision is blurred, there is a horrifying sense of mortality hanging everywhere. She muses, "She had the kiss of death on her. You could see the marks. Mortality infested her, she was a carrier, it was catching. She lay there thinking... Life is just another sexually transmitted social disease" (BH, p. 201). Rennie, like Som Bhaskar in Arun Joshi's _The Last Labyrinth_ and Maya in Anita Desai's _Cry, the Peacock,_ is haunted by the death neurosis.

> _Rennie decided she was being silly and possibly neurotic as well. She didn't want to turn into the sort of woman who was afraid of men. It's your own fear of death, she told herself. That's what any armchair shrink would tell you. You think you're dying, even though you've been saved. You should be grateful, you should be serene and profound, but instead you're projecting onto some pathetic weirdo who's never going to bother you again (BH, pp. 40-41)._

Urooj Abdi in _Death Anxiety_ says that "Death anxiety" is related to "the Purpose in life". It is "an integral part of the cognitive motivational structure of the anxiety neurotic personality."[5] The absence of meaning or a disturbance in the meaning system of an individual only accentuates the death anxiety. Both Rennie and Arun Joshi's Som lose the meaning of life as they are rejected by their lovers. Anuradha vanishes, leaving Som in a shock and Jake rejects Rennie, which lands her in a vacuum.

Since Rennie defines herself in relation to Jake, his rejection devastates her. When he strikes against her feelings, she feels neglected, abused and it reinforces her clinging attitude: she alternately glorifies him and scorns him for being a self-righteous and proud narcissist. Her attitude towards such maltreatment is full of contradictions and leads her into more and more conflict. To begin with, she is simply helpless and pretends not to see the reality of the operation and lets Jake also pretend that everything is normal. For that she has to make an unbearable effort. She also resorts to rationalisation, that their relationship was without strings and commitment. Failure was, therefore, out of their "terms of reference." This rationalisation does not hold ground when Jake blows her pride by saying that she is of no use to him now. This makes her feel guilty. And being prone to feeling guilty she rather agrees with him, though his reproaches shatter her self-image. She responds to his treatment by becoming anxious, despondent or desperate, but she does not fight back. She hopes to win him by the appeal of passivity and on the ground of love. Thus she insists on "quiet companionship" (BH, p. 101) and talks of "life-long goals" (BH, p. 126). Jake's reactions are contrary to her expectations, "if you don't like the road, don't go, said Jake, smiling at her. I'm not too good at life-time goals" (BH, p. 126). He disregards her wishes to have babies. To Jake, having babies means to restrict one's choices. "You don't want to limit your options too soon, said Jake, as if it was only her options that would be limited, it had nothing to do with him" (BH, p. 126).

Being a morbidly dependent person, she cannot openly express her rage at his ill-treatment which spurts in indirect ways, in complaints, suffering, martyrdom and an increased desire to cling. But Jake shatters all her pretences. "I'm not a mind man. I'm more interested in your body, if you want the truth" (BH, p. 104). He makes her ashamed of herself by withdrawing physically and psychically. He shocks her when he flaunts his relationship with another woman. That she has been merely a sexual object to him is nauseating for her, because it reduces her identity to zero.

Feminist critics view this as a male principle and correlate the fragmented or fractured identity with patriarchal tendency to break up and divide everything into polar opposites. Thus Elizabeth, Auntie Muriel, Peter, Arthur and all "male" principles in her novels divide the world into violent dualities. Jake too, like a typical male, sees Rennie in part-mind and body, rather than a whole person and though he adores her body, he does not acknowledge or care that she has a mind. For Jake "a packager", Rennie is a thing he can arrange and package. As Rennie says, "It took her more time than it should have, to realize that she was one of the things Jake was packaging" (BH, p. 104). He "liked thinking of sex as something he could win at." Jake's attitude symbolically constitutes the typical male-view of a woman that inferiorises the woman and thereby problematises feminine identity. What Nandine in Joyce Carol Oates's *Them* says about women's lot may well be quoted here:

> *A woman is like a dream. Her life is a dream of waiting. I mean she lives in a dream waiting for a man. There's no way out of this insulting as it is, no woman can escape it. Her life is a waiting for a man. That's all. There is a certain door in this dream and she has to walk through it… She has no choice.*[6]

We are not working out a parallel here, but only trying to show how men use women. Women writers are aware of this victim position which damages their self-esteem. Atwood's heroines also feel dissatisfied and trapped, and have the urge to run away.

This feminist interpretation can be substantiated with the help of psychological tenets of Horney. Rennie, the rejected beloved is feeling hurt. She hates herself as a loser. Her image is crushed, "I feel like a blank sheet of paper, she said. For you to doodle on" (BH, p. 105). She feels "useless" and reacts to this recognition with self-contempt and suffers the insult of rejection. According to Horney, "a rejection is an insult for anybody whose pride is largely invested in making everybody love him" (NHG, p. 245). When Jake broke off their relationship, Rennie was thrown into the turmoil of despair and shock, particularly because he discarded her by saying that he did not want to go on with her after this operation. "When Jake moved out, naturally there was a vacuum. Something had to come in to fill it" (BH, p. 39). Horney emphatically maintains that morbidly dependent person cannot stand being alone. The narrator makes it look like a normal characteristic of the people of Griswold, her childhood home. "People in Griswold, had a great fear of being left alone. It was supposed to be bad for you, it made you go funny, it drove you bats" (BH, p. 109). But to say that Rennie is affected by this general characteristic of the people of her town is to reduce her problem to a simplistic formula. Hers is an individual case and need to be understood in relation with her psychology.

The gap made by Jake's exit is filled in by Daniel. Fromm corroborates Horney by saying that if one relation ends with separation, it "is usually followed by the choice of another object who is expected to fulfill all hopes connected with the magic helper" (pp. 175-77). Fromm's account resembles Rennie's morbid dependency on Jake which is followed by her relation with Daniel. Now Daniel is expected to fulfil all her hopes connected with the magic helper. He provides her safety and saves her from fear of exposure which has badly affected her psyche. Rennie rationalises that with the doctor, there is no fear of exposure as he already knows her inside out and it was "safe, there was absolutely nothing he could demand." In order to rationalise her new relationship she asserts to herself that she fell in love with the doctor because he knows something about "her she doesn't know, he knows what she's like inside" (BH, p. 81). Moreover, Daniel is "fantasy for her: a fantasy about the lack of fantasy, a fantasy of the normal" (BH, p. 237). Daniel also acknowledges this relationship, "I'm a fantasy for you. It's normal" (BH, p. 101). He, too, is dependent on her emotionally. Fromm says that if the helpers are also dependents, it strengthens "the impression" that this relationship is one of "real love."

Daniel is also a self-effacing man and he wants an escape, "a little but not too much, a window but not a door" (BH, p. 195). He admits that he is fond of Rennie but neurotic compulsions would not let him express it. "I'm not good at that sort of thing, Daniel said. I'd resent you for it and I don't want that. I care about you, I care what happens to you. I guess I think I can do more for you as your doctor; I' m better at it" (BH, p. 196). But Rennie is not satisfied with this, she has an aggressive urge for sexual union with him:

> She wanted to lie down beside him and touch him and be touched by him; at the moment she believed in it, the touch of the hand that could transform you, change everything, magic. She wanted to see him lying with his eyes closed, she wanted to see him and not be seen, she wanted to be trusted. She wanted to make love with him, very slowly, she wanted it to last a long time, she wanted the moment just before coming, helplessness, hours of it, she wanted to open him up (BH, pp. 195-96).

In terms of Freud, her persistent demands for physical intimacy can be called "oral erotic." But when interpreted from Horneyan tenets, "Sexual relations may stand out as the only satisfactory contact... Sex may mean for her the only assurance of love" (NHG, p. 250). Not only this, she gets a feeling of being "wanted." Both Daniel and Rennie are unsure of their needs for love. As Rennie remarks "she wasn't sure whether she wanted it or not, an affair with Daniel" (BH, p. 155). It was not a question of their wishing it. Both being dependents have neurotic needs for love. Both are needy. Here is the love that says "I love you because I need you." Erich Fromm terms it "immature love." It does not give the sense of sharing and openness rather it produces a feeling of dependency. Fromm and Horney acknowledge the possibility that both parties may be dependents. Here is the case of mutual morbid dependency, although Rennie is far more enslaved than Daniel. Their neurotic needs and compulsions clash and produce much of Rennie's emotional turmoil and generate intense anxiety and self-hate.

Neurotic pride is the enemy of love and that is why Daniel recoils from touch or physical nearness. He refuses to go to bed with her and gives the reason that "It would be unethical, he said. I'd be taking advantage of you. You're in an emotional state" (BH, p. 143). If we probe into the psychological reasons for this, we see that Daniel is living up to his "shoulds": a married man "should" not go for extra-marital relations. If he acts contrary to it, he would be shattering his neurotic pride and falling a prey to self-hate. Keeping a safe distance from Rennie is his strategy to guard his neurotic pride. As for Rennie, she fails to understand Daniel's psyche. Daniel's approach tantamounts to rejection. She is probably a "vacation" which he thinks "he shouldn't have taken. She felt like a straw that had been clutched, she felt he'd been drowning. She felt raped" (BH, p. 238). She was ashamed of herself for falling in love with the married man which ordinarily middle aged married women do. That she has been refused and rejected is further unbearably shameful. Under the grip of self-contempt, she berates herself as an "event, a freak." She cannot accept the fact that Daniel is needy like her and ashamed of like her. She feels revolted to accept that he needs the same compassion and understanding. Horney is of the opinion that it is natural for a compliant person to dislike another compliant one. In this sense, Rennie's reaction to Daniel's behaviour and needs is natural. She muses, "He had no right to appeal to her like that, to throw himself on her mercy. She wasn't God, she didn't have to be understanding..." (BH, p. 196). True to her compliant character, she fails either to forgive him or believe in his needs:

> *The fact was that he had needed something from her, which she could neither believe nor forgive. She'd been counting on him not to: she was supposed to be the needy one, but it was the other way around. He was ashamed of himself, which was the last thing she'd wanted (BH, p. 238).*

Rennie cannot commit herself to others selflessly because she lacks faith in herself. Fromm observes that in such cases "while one is consciously afraid of not being loved, the real, though unconscious fear is that of loving. To love means to commit oneself without guarantee."[8] When Daniel does not show intimacy, she blames him for being needy. She has ingrained in herself the habit of blaming others for her calamities. In her childhood, when she was unable to feel what she was supposed to, she would blame her mother. She also blamed her father for leaving her behind in her mother's care. Then it was Jake and Daniel and later it was her body. Her self alienation is at its height when she considers her body separate from herself. She feels it is her enemy and feels outraged and hurls accusation at the body: "feeling that she'd been betrayed by a close friend. She'd given her body swimming twice a week, forbidden it junk food and cigarette smoke, allowed it a normal amount of sexual release. She'd trusted it. Why then had it turned against her?" (BH, p. 82). While blaming her body, she is externalising her self-hate. Thus it is revealed that she is not only alienated from her body but also is impaired emotionally. It has affected her spontaneity and sensibility. She confesses to Daniel, "I don't feel human any more..." (BH, p. 83). Even her breast cancer with its obvious serious implications becomes merely a possible subject for her lifestyle's columns and she thinks she could do a piece on it, "Cancer, The Coming Thing" (BH, p. 27). This shows that her fears of Bodily Harm have a strong hold on her.

Apparently, the title *Bodily Harm* stands for Rennie's breast cancer, "the way she was damaged, amputated" (BH, p. 198). One scholar views it not only as a plot device but also as a metaphor for a malignant world. The disease really to be feared, Rennie comes to realise, is "the capacity to take pleasure from another's pain." To Linda Hutcheon in *Bodily Harm*, "themes of violation –

physical, psychological and ideological – "[10] are the focus for Atwood. Rennie feels not only violated physically but also "raped" in her relationship and psychologically she is deeply affected. She has started associating herself with something rotten and malignant. "So it's my fault if there's a recurrence? I have cancer of the mind? said Rennie" (BH, p. 82). The novelist highlights Rennie's fear of exposure and how she associates her disease with "maggots," "diseased fruit." A clear picture of Rennie's psyche is provided in terms of various motifs, dreams and other recurring symbols of bodily harm such as: centipedes and maggots. "I feel infested... I'm full of white maggots eating away at me from the inside" (BH, p. 83). The centipedes relate her with the kind of thing she has been having bad dreams about. Her obsessive fears grip her. She remarks, "Her real fear, irrational but a fear, is that the scar will come undone in the water, split open like a faulty zipper, and she will turn inside out" (BH, p. 80). Her resemblance to "split fish" and "infested body" are linked by the central metaphor of the title *Bodily Harm*. It is indicative of her morbidity due to her fears and its various manifestations, the ingrained fears of death are at the bottom of her weird dreams.

Rennie's emotional withdrawal has become so complete that her grandmother's delusion is now her own nightmare. Shannon Hengen calls it Rennie's "regressive narcissism. One sign of which is repression of feelings associated with intimacy, vulnerability, interconnection."[11] In her dreams, she is searching for lost hands. Rennie dreams, she is "rummaging through her slips, scarves, sweaters... It's her hands she is looking for, she knows she left them here somewhere, folded neatly in a drawer, like gloves" (BH, p. 116). The search for lost hands in dreams can be interpreted as her search for lost identity and cancer stands for a threat to her whole self.

The operative surgery for her breast cancer metaphorically reinforces the idea of Rennie's incompleteness – like her grandmother's. Images of severance and sawing off in physical terms symbolically point to Rennie's fractured identity. The memory of her grandmother's "lost" hands further reinforces the idea of Rennie's incomplete identity. The memory of her stern and heartless grandmother who pries away young Rennie's hands "finger by finger" (BH, p. 53) and shuts her up in cellar where, "there were things... that might get on you and run up your legs"

(BH, p. 53) impinges upon adult Rennie's consciousness. As a child, Rennie learns three important things: "how to be quiet, what not to say, and how to look at things without touching them" (BH, p. 54) and to "keep her options open." She defines herself against Griswold, "Griswold is ingrained in her mind" (BH, p. 118). Her Griswold syndrome is: "If you can't say anything nice, don't say anything at all." "If you can't keep your word, don't give it." The meaning of life to Rennie lies not in the realisation of self but in the realisation of these Griswold values.

According to a scholar, "Griswold does not offer commentary but it does help to define the absences or lacunae in Rennie's personality."[12] It would be appropriate to point out here that in Margaret Laurence's novels, women relate themselves to Makawana – macrocosm of cultural heritage to gain identity and self-definition. But Rennie's Griswold was a place without compassion and the old Victorian house of her childhood is a place of emotional withholding without touching or intimacy. It is related to the memory of her grandmother who has lost her hands. "My other hands" as she says, "The ones I had before, the ones I touch things with" (BH, p. 57). The grandmother, like Elizabeth in *Life Before Man*, is a woman who embodies the forces of repression and domination that account for Rennie's passivity and subservience. The grandmother has problematised her perception and self-perception. Rennie views herself without any worth. Her prominent wish is not to displease her grandmother, in case, she had inadvertently displeased her, she insists on her forgiveness. Karen Horney categorically refers to these 'injurious influences' which prevent a child from arriving at a correct self-evaluation. In addition to Griswold's Puritanical culture, and the grandmother's influences, the saintly performance of Rennie's mother greatly affect her psyche. Rennie recalls: "everyone was always telling me how admirable she was, she was practically a saint – I didn't want to be like her in anyway" (BH, p. 58). Karen Horney elaborates such influences, she remarks, "A rigid regime of perfectionist standards [saintly] may evoke in him a feeling of inferiority for not measuring up to such demands... Moves towards autonomy or independence may be ridiculed" (NHG, p. 87). This alienated Rennie from her mother's world. Early in life, she stopped telling her mother the "bad news," since her mother does not understand her and regard such things not as accidents but as acts Rennie committed on purpose to complicate her mother's life. Hence she refrains from telling her about such a traumatic experience of her operation and Jake's decision. Rennie believes that the "operation, too, she [her mother] would see as Rennie's fault" (BH, p. 82) and "something you brought upon yourself" (BH, p. 82).

In reality, her mother has her own psychological compulsions. She shows her neurotic urge to win over Rennie and her sympathy when she breaks the news of her husband's betrayal. This can be termed as the need to get "nurturing" from the daughter. Feminist psychologist Nancy Chodorow, P. Caplan, Juliet Mitchell and Alice Miller have studied women's need for "nurturing" which they feel, is a kind of projection – the mother-daughter identification. This pattern is manifested in the role reversal between mother and daughter. The under-nurtured mother looks to her own daughter for reinforcement and validation. This is injurious to the daughter's life as it demands "sweet compliance" and "good girl" behaviour. Caplan argues in her study *Barriers Between Women*[13] that mothers who are themselves overburdened with family responsibilities and have been under-nurtured as daughters will push aside their own daughters' needs to get nurtured as least important and most troublesome. Karen Horney in her diary describes her relationship with her mother. Her attitude is often protective which is expressed in her phrase "poor little mutti."[14] Explaining a woman's need for nurturing and its ill effects on the daughter, Marcia WestCott terms it as "female altruism" which is ultimately damaging for the girl child. This is damaging for Rennie too. It killed in her the natural urges for growth and creativity. She did not want to become a mother:

> I didn't want to be like her in anyway, I didn't want to have a family or be anyone's mother, ever; I had none of those ambitions. I didn't want to own many objects or inherit any. I didn't want to cope. I didn't want to deteriorate. I used to pray that I wouldn't live long enough to get like my grandmother, and now I guess I won't (BH, p. 58).

Happy marriage and internalising gender-role of creativity are the secret of feminine fulfilment. But, Rennie cannot enact such a role without internal conflict that is partly a reflection of her "basic anxiety." To Rennie they tantamount to traps in which women like her mother get caught. As far as she is concerned, she refuses to fall a victim to these societal traps. However, she is trapped, "One man I'm not allowed to touch, she thought, and another I won't allow to touch me" (BH, p. 198). Rennie has an exaggerated opinion of herself which falsifies reality. She has not learnt how to cope up with reality, this produces much of her emotional and intellectual turmoil. Rennie's claims clamoured for extra-special treatment from fate. Realising that fate is relentless and it has struck her, comes to her as a blow. "Rennie had not intended to have a life crisis and she did not feel in need of support. But now she did" (BH, p. 163). This makes her vulnerable; that she is ordinary and liable to be buffeted by fate is unacceptable to her. Moreover, she cannot accept the fact that the men in her life are ordinary. Atwood's heroines hate putting up with mediocre heroes who want ordinary joys of life and lead ordinary life... Rennie is shocked to realise that "she'd fallen in love with, the absolutely ordinary raised to the degree of X" (BH, pp. 196-197). Daniel with his ordinariness offends Rennie. When she realises that she herself is mediocre, she "couldn't stand being guilty of such a banality". To live the life of an ordinary human is beyond the scope of her neurotic claim.

Self hate is the logical outcome of a conflict between Rennie's pride system and her real self. The result is that she has scorn for herself. She sees herself as an "idiot" "a hypocrite" (BH, p. 137) "fraudulent" (BH, p. 227), "dumb, gullible, naive" to believe people. "She feels superfluous and both invisible and exposed: something so much there that nobody looks at it" (BH, p. 233). Her expansive side wants her to master this negative image; to do something about it. At this time, it is her neurotic need to present herself as normal. To satisfy this need, she looks into the mirror and wants it to approve her as a normal person. Hengen remarks, Rennie's "mirror stage is the most prolonged and dangerous but also potentially the most effective of those experienced by Atwood's central females."[15] "Unlike Marian, however Rennie starts her movement towards self-knowledge in that state of disorientation beyond or behind mirrors." Mirror becomes her glorified self. As in the case of Conrad's "The Secret Sharer," Rennie's secret image merges with the mirrored self. She examines her face in the mirror checking for signs and she feels satisfied when she looks normal.

A normal person does not need to put a "shiny new lock" on her past as Rennie does. She also avoids thinking of her future. She lives in present that also on surfaces. When she cannot face realities in the present, the only alternative is to escape. She is convinced that "failure is easy to avoid. All you have to do is walk away" (BH, p. 203). Unable to cope with what seems an increasingly threatened existence in Toronto, Rennie attempts an escape. She ends with an adventurous assignment on the Caribbean islands, "she had never heard off." She escapes to the Caribbean island to take "small absences from real life" (BH, p. 16) and from her past "since out was where she needed to be" (BH, p. 16). Thus she makes a move away from people. She adopts the strategy of detachment, withdrawal. She protects herself by renouncing her desires. "She had given up expecting anything..." (BH, p. 237) she feels that was the right way to do it, never to expect anything. She flaunts her "who cares" attitude with Dr Minnow, Lora and Paul. This solution is not without satisfaction. Not only does it protect her against self-hate which she incurs when she does something foolish but also feeds her pride. This is reflected in her remarks that "she can make her own choices, she doesn't need to have them made for her" (BH, p. 234). She is ready to pay the price by stopping all human communication. Now she does not want to start a conversation. Conversations lead to acquaintances and "acquaintances are too easy to make on these trips. People mistake them for friendships" (BH, p. 88). She refuses herself this.

She believes in the possibility of being "away... invisible... safe." But the reality of the situation is that rather being invisible, she is watched wherever she goes. In a place where corruption and unbridled power mean that "nothing is inconceivable" (BH, p. 133), Rennie learns that there is no such thing as safety, "neutrality" and "invisibility;" once for all she abandons the notion that "she's tourist, she's exempt" (BH, p. 203). In Caribbean island "massive involvement" becomes unavoidable. Paul sees the change, "you're getting too involved," (BH, p. 234) he says. This helps her to recover and define herself alone in relation to men and women she meets amidst the violent political upheaval on St Antoine. That is why a critic says that "Essentially the plot is about recovery." Rennie recovers her capacity for sexual pleasure in a brief affair with a small town, local drug runner—Paul.

Though, "She knows nothing about him, she doesn't need to know anything, he knows nothing about her, it is perfect" (BH, p. 100). For her, "love is tangled, sex is straight" (BH, p. 223) and she knows her urgency for sexual intimacy. "This is something she wants to do, again, finally, she wants it so much her hands are shaking" (BH, p. 100). This is an unhealthy drive to achieve mastery of life, but in the case of Rennie, she owes it to Paul for giving back her body. She no longer feels untouchable. It is the beginning of her attempt to participate in life at large.

Rennie's ritualistic reaching out like Elizabeth in *Life Before Man*, recovers her capacity for compassion in her relationship with Lora. Lora is Rennie's cellmate after Minnow's assassination, they are put in the jail as subversives. Lora is also an Ontarian, living on St Antoine and is vulnerable to men, she has become involved with "Prince," who is the second opposition candidate. Lora and Rennie are "unlikely companions." In contrast to Rennie's middle class upbringing, Lora is the child of poverty and abuse. Lora is street-wise while Rennie is university-educated. To hardened Lora, sexual favours to the guards are simply survival tactics. It is "not any different from having some guy stick his finger in your ear" (BH, p. 286), but to Rennie, "it isn't decent." It is repelling like her hands which are dirty, finger nails bitten to the quick and the skin chewed. But Lora's passionate love for the leader of political uprising, Prince, and her eventual brutalisation by the police force are seen by Rennie with open eyes. At last, against her will Rennie is doing what Minnow has asked her to, "look with eyes open." "She doesn't want to see, she has to see, why isn't someone covering her eyes?" (BH, p. 293). She wanted to feel compassion but she could not. "She looks down at her hands, which ought to contain comfort. Compassion. She ought to go over to Lora and put her arms around her and pat her on the back, but she can't" (BH, p. 286). As Lora lies senseless on the prison floor, Rennie takes her hand believing that if she tries hard enough "Something will move and live again, something will get born" (BH, p. 299).

Holding Lora, Rennie acknowledges that her healing is a "gift." The gift of healing is related to women's enduring and unspoken powers in the character of Elva, the Caribbean grandmother and masseuse who informs Rennie that the "magic" (BH, p. 194) of her hands is a "gift I have... from my grandmother... She pass it to me" (BH, p. 193). Shannon is of the opinion that "in order to find the renewed identity," Rennie has to "empower the goodness which both her matrilineage and national history provide by joining it to subversive writing."[16] Stouck sees in this compassion of Rennie for Lora "the new stance" in picturing one woman helping another woman. Only in the collection titled *Two Headed Poems* (1978) does Atwood picture the joining together of women and there it is in terms of matriarchal lineage. He remarks, "In her novels to date there is no female tradition, no warm female friendships, no nurturing mother figures or places to call home, only enemies and alien territory. Rennie reaching out to Lora may seem more hypothetical than actual, but its significance should not be dismissed."[17] Another critic asserts that at the end of the novel "we don't know whether Rennie has accomplished a miracle, only that she has tried. "[18] This "trying" itself is significant because in doing so she has learnt to reach out to others.

Whether she accomplishes a miracle or whether she still fantasises are not important. But that there is a change in her perception which is the point of importance: "What she sees has not altered; only the way she sees it" (BH, p. 300). Right perception is the beginning of a right action. She is showing the right perception in her altered attitude towards life and death. It is revealed in her understanding that she can no longer ignore the faceless strangers in the world crying for help, "there's no such thing as a faceless stranger, every face is someone's, it has a name" (BH, p. 299). This knowledge not only frees her from aloof detachment towards others but also releases in her for the first time "genuine compassion for the hurts and sufferings of her fellow beings."[19] Thus she reaffirms her allegiance to humanity and symbolically she regains her identity as a whole human being. In the enlarged understanding of life, she accepts death personified as the stranger with the rope. Thus she is relieved of her death-neurosis and accepts the mortality of the body. "Nobody lives for ever, who said you could?" (BH, p. 204) and realises "who was at the end" (BH, p. 41) of the rope.

In Maslowian terminology it is "B-Cognition." "In B-cognition, the experience or the object (experienced) tends to be seen as... detached from relations, from possible usefulness, from expediency, and from purpose..." Maslow often used the phrases "peak-experience" and "B-cognition" interchangeably. Just as a self-actualising person sees reality more clearly as a *matter of course*, so does the ordinary person see it more clearly in his peak experience. It is seen in "itself and for itself." Rennie, being an ordinary person, sees it in peak experience in jail. It is not compared or evaluated or judged, it is simply beheld, that is what Rennie has done. In William Golding's *Free Fall*, the protagonist Sammy Mountjoy has a peak experience in a cell in the German camp, which changes his perception. It infuses one who has it, says Maslow with "a profound sense of humility, smallness, unworthiness before the enormity of experience."[20] This is exactly how Rennie feels: that her suffering and scar are insignificant. She is reconciled. "She may be dying, true, but if so she's doing it slowly," relatively speaking. She accepts her fate, not under compulsion but after reaching understanding of the human situation.

Towards the end, this experience has changed Rennie from a woman who "can't make a sound" (BH, p. 293) of protest when Lora is beaten, to a woman who is resolved to be a "reporter." All strategies Rennie adopted to achieve "neutrality" and "invisibility" have been dropped. She fantasises about her release from the prison but in fantasy also she is thinking of reality: she will report if she survives, "the way she sees it." She is filled with positive thoughts and power of emotional bonding. She is lucky if she is released, if not, no outside force has the power to break her. She has emerged "unharmed" and suffers from no fear of death or mortality. A man/woman is known by the choice he/she makes. She has chosen her future.

References

1. Annette Kolodny, "Margaret Atwood and the Politics of Narrative," in *Studies on Canadian Literature*. ed. Arnold E Davidson, p. 97.

2. Linda Hutcheon, *The Canadian Postmodern*, p. 153.

3. Margaret Atwood, address delivered at a conference "Imagined Realities in contemporary women writing," Dyffryn House near Cardiff (October, 1982) organised by the Welsh Arts council.

4. Erich Fromm, *Escape from Freedom*, p. 175.

5. Urooj Abdi, *Death Anxiety* (New Delhi: Radha Publication, 1990), pp. 79-80.

6. Joyce Carol Oates, *Them* (New York: The Vanguard Press, 1969) p. 367.

7. Erich Fromm, *Escape from Freedom*, pp. 175-77.

8. Erich Fromm, *The Art of Living*, p. 105.

9. Annette Kolodny, "Margaret Atwood and The Politics of Narrative," in *Studies on Canadian Literature*, p. 232.

10. Linda Hutcheon, *The Canadian Postmodern*, p. 153.

11. Shannon Hengen, *Margaret Atwood's Power*, p. 95.

12. Annette Kolodny, "Margaret Atwood and The Politics of Narrative," p. 100.

13. P. Caplan, *Barriers Between Women* (Jamaica, New York: Spectrum Publications, 1981).

14. Karen Horney, *The Adolescent Diaries of Karen Horney* (New York: Basic Books, 1980), p. 42.

15. Shannon Hengen, *Margaret Atwood's Power*, p. 89.

16. Shannon Hengen, p. 94.

17. David Stouck, *Major Canadian Authors*, p. 290.

18. Jerome H. Rosenberg, p. 133.

19. David Stouck, *Major Canadian Authors*, p. 290.

20. Abraham H. Maslow, *Psychology of Being*, p. 77.

CHAPTER 7

Cat's Eye

In the preceding chapters, we discussed the psychological compulsions of five women protagonists, namely, Marian in *The Edible Woman*, the narrator-heroine of *Surfacing*, Joan Foster in *Lady Oracle*, Elizabeth and Lesje in *Life Before Man* and Rennie in *Bodily Harm*, and tried to gain insight into their behaviour. The analysis revealed the psychologically intelligible heroines striving to grapple with the crisis which elude solution. The protagonist of *Cat's Eye* is not much different from her earlier counterparts. Like them she shifts the blame on others and tries to convince herself and her readers that Cordelia has been the cause of her troubles. In this connection, it would be relevant to refer to the heroine of *Surfacing* who is sure that her parents and her lover have created problems for her; Joan Foster squarely blames her mother; and Marian shifts the responsibility on Peter. This strategy relieves them of tension and saves them from self-hate. Another strategy which all except Joan Foster adopt is of running away and returning back. The motion is thus circular. The protagonist of *Surfacing* returns to the lake-side abode in search of her father and relives her past; Marian accepts her life after making Peter eat the cake; Joan does not return but we have every reason to believe she would; and Elaine recasts her past after coming back to Toronto. In the process she not only blows Cordelia into an out of proportion bully and herself as a victim but she also reveals her own psychological conflicts, perpetuated by her inability to wriggle out of her past. Her theory is that one does not "look back along time but down through it, like water" (CE, p. 3). The very act of looking "down through it" suggests plumbing the depth. In other words, it is introspective, whereas Elaine professes to have returned to Toronto for a "Retrospective" of her paintings. The novel thus works on two levels—retrospection and introspection—which provide some base to understand Elaine's epistemological problems despite the phenomenological data made available by the "unreliable" first person narrator.

The first person narrator replays in her mind the fragmented pieces of her childhood and reconstructs her life. Soon the picture of Toronto of her childhood is complete with her brother Stephen teasing her, her mother engaged in a constant battle to transform her into an acceptable girl child and her friend Cordelia bullying her into accepting the norms of Toronto society. Elaine grows into an adult with a damaged sense of personal worth. It is only when she is away from Toronto that her art flowers. When she returns to her childhood surrounding as a middle-aged painter after many years of absence, she finds herself "rampant with memory" like Hagar Shipley of Margaret Laurence's *The Stone Angel*.[1] But unlike Hagar, she does not rage about time. Instead, she realises that "time has a dimension" and that "nothing goes away" from memory. In Elaine's memory, Cordelia reigns supreme as a fearful presence because she has had the ability to reduce Elaine to "nothing," to make her "rigid with anxiety" (CE, p. 124). In Cordelia's presence she feels "without worth, that nothing I can do is of any value, least of all to myself" (CE, p. 41). With her brother Stephen trying to educate her, so that she does not become "a pin-headed fuzzbrain" (CE, p. 218) and Cordelia always ready to frighten her by her overbearing presence, we get the self portrait of Elaine as a "nut." There is always "a force" (CE, p. 373) pushing her to do things as others want them done. She feels "locked in" (CE, p. 400), a victim, a will-less creature, mute and faceless.

The themes of the novel, one of mental journey across time, and another of victimisation are established by the two epigraphs. The first, from *Memory of Fire: Genesis,* reads thus:

> When the Tukanas cut off her head, the old woman collected her own blood in her hands and blew it towards the sun. 'My soul enters you too!' she shouted. Since then anyone who kills, receives in his body, without wanting or knowing it, the soul of his victim.

This epigraph is relevant for us to analyse Elaine's crisis. Has Elaine killed Cordelia? If yes, how and why? If no, then, why is she overburdened by her spirit? It seems from her childhood memories that Cordelia has been important in the formation of

Elaine's identity. In the chapters describing Elaine in the present as an artist, we learn about her adult life and the haunting effect of her dual identity. If Elaine and Cordelia are "like the twins in the old fables, each of whom has been given half a key" (CE, p. 411), it follows that Cordelia is in Horneyan terminology, the "arrogant-vindictive" side of self-effacing Elaine. The conflict, thus, is not between Cordelia and Elaine, but between the two contradictory drives. The other problem is articulated by the novelist in her second epigraph: "Why do we remember the past, and not the future?" Elaine's inability to wriggle free of her haunting past makes her vulnerable and self-denigrating. The process of retrospection and introspection produces tension between the theme and the mimesis which accounts for much of the beauty of Atwood's realism. That is why many critics classify the novel as "autobiographical" or "transparent autobiography"[2] and trace Elaine Risley's "resemblance to Atwood." If a "retrospective" is "a point of arrival, or a plateau that provides a view of the past – a reflective pause – before one moves into the future,"[3] then Elaine's "Retrospective" of her paintings should resolve the crisis voiced by the second epigraph. Moving from the past into future should purge Elaine Risley of her self-accusation and self-denigration and make her "an autonomous and independent"[4] artist, as Martha Sharpe views her. Our purpose here is to *see through* the protagonist and not *at her* as she presents herself, so as to grasp all the aspects of her personality. For this we shall seek help from her story. When we dive down time "Sometimes this comes to the surface, sometimes that, sometimes nothing" (CE, p. 3). What "comes to the surface" will promise the clue to her innermost self.

According to the protagonist, the two forces which affected her psyche and undermined her basic self-confidence are: her changed social milieu and the negative influence of Cordelia. She feels alien and apprehensive when the family settles down in Toronto, after years of wandering. Till now, she and her brother have led "an old rootless life of impermanence and safety" but it was a happy life. Toronto with its new environment threatens her. Significantly, chapter II opens with a categorical statement, "Until we moved to Toronto I was happy" (CE, p. 21). It gives a graphic picture of her happy childhood, before she was nine. It was the life of "nomads on the far edges of the war" (CE, p. 25) driving long distances with the packed household, living in tents, in motels and enjoying the warmth of brother-sister relationship. But once they settle down in Toronto, things change for little Elaine. Her meeting with Cordelia, "lanky, sinewy," with "a smile like a grownup's," (CE, p. 70) overwhelms her. Suddenly she feels helpless and unhappy and looks for safety and reassurance. At school, Mrs Lumley "rules by fear," the social microcosm terrifies her.

Here, the children are divided into categories of boys and girls with separate entry points and secret codes of language. Untrained in the ways of the world, Elaine feels "awkward" with her girl friends. "I know the unspoken rules of boys, but with girls I sense that I am always on the verge of some unforeseen, calamitous blunder" (CE, p. 47). Socially, the family feels alien in stifling middle-class world of Toronto. More so Elaine, whose friends marvel at her as if she were a museum piece, an "exotic" item, someone who is not one of them but an outsider landed in their midst "from outside the city" (CE, p. 49). When Carol tells others in school about the way the Risleys live, she makes it sound as if "she's reporting on the antics of some primitive tribe: true, but incredible" (CE, p. 49). Carol, Grace and Cordelia, girls from affluent middle-class families influence little Elaine. Her constant effort is to measure up to their standards so that she becomes "acceptable" to them. Being "acceptable" becomes of foremost importance to Elaine because it means being "lovable." In order to be lovable, she experiences herself as her subdued, victimised self—small, helpless and vulnerable. This, according to Horney, is the "shrinking process" (NHG, p. 223). "Everything will be all right as long as I sit still, say nothing, reveal nothing, I will be saved then, I will be acceptable..." (CE, p. 117). By thus reducing herself to a zero, she hopes to minimise her anxiety born out of the fear of rejection.

The conditions for and the symptoms of anxiety take roots in Elaine's home. The atmosphere of non-conformity of her home is socially and culturally alienating. She is constantly haunted by the fear of being put to shame for not belonging to any church. Her father's liberal ideas about bringing up children and his belief that religion "has been responsible for a lot of wars and massacres... as well as bigotry and intolerance" (CE, p. 96), do not equip Elaine to face her friends and their religious church-going parents. It is not complimentary when Mrs Smeath looks at her "as if I'm an orphan left on her doorstep" (CE, p. 97) or when Aunt Mildred derides her as a "heathen" or when her friends mock at her. The highbrow Toronto neighbourhood makes her aware of her parent's monetary position. Compared to Carol, Grace and Cordelia whose mothers wear "rubber gloves while washing dishes" (CE, p. 51), who sleep on new-fashioned twin-beds with matching "chenille bedspreads" and who can spend "money on flowers".

Elaine's parents are plain middle-class people who have led an unsettled, nomadic life. Seeing the glory and glamour around, Elaine realises "for the first time that we are not rich" (CE, p. 71). This gives a blow to her self-esteem. In order to salvage it, she "doles" out gifts, which she terms as "offerings" and "atonements" and feels happy because "just before giving, I am loved" (CE, p. 135). This is her moment of triumph, it ensures company and since as a self-effacing person she cannot "stand being alone" (NHG, p. 227), human contact and company is of paramount importance to give meaning to her existence.

Existence for Elaine is both defined and limited by her image of herself as viewed by Cordelia. She is often attacked as "stupid," "mute" and "alien." So powerful is the impact of Cordelia on Elaine's psyche that she is unable to see herself as an independent entity. Even as a middle-aged painter she is not free of the image, which sometimes chokes her; sometimes it frightens her; and often it haunts her. As the author herself substantiates it, the novel is "partly about being haunted"[5] not only by the past but also by her own obsessive thoughts. Adult Elaine is disturbed by Cordelia's ever-present spirit. She hears her voice "inviting and conspiratorial, gleeful, urging me over" (CE, p. 375), saying "Do it. Come on. Do it" (CE, p. 373) and under its impact Elaine slashes her wrist with a knife. "This voice doesn't offer a choice; it has the force of an order" (CE, p. 373), it rings inside her head and becomes her secret Cordelia, thus becomes a part of her self. She cannot shrug her off.

Drawing a parallel between Lear's Cordelia in Shakespeare and Elaine's Cordelia in *Cat's Eye*, a critic considers it a case of "an arrested state of the mirror stage" in which the child identifies with the parent in viewing his or her own identity. In the case of both Lear and Elaine, Cordelia becomes the reintegrated presence. "Unable to rid themselves of the image of Cordelia, they live with split or dual identities – Cordelia fills and defines their other halves."[6] Elaine is only her half-self without Cordelia. Even her self-portrait has only the upper half. Cordelia's portrait is named *Half a Face*. She, thus, is fragmented without Cordelia. In Horneyan terminology Cordelia is Elaine's "expansive self" existing with her compliant strategy of defence. Since Elaine is narrator she has the advantage of projecting herself as she sees and feels. She considers herself a sufferer, a victim and would like her readers to believe her, but despite our sympathy for her and with her, we understand that she is adopting a defensive measure to ward off her inner conflicts by throwing the blame on Cordelia.

We agree that Cordelia is responsible to an extent for damaging child Elaine's self-confidence, but to let her victimiser engulf a part of her identity and to let herself be crippled for life is an indication of Elaine's psychological weakness. Elaine narrates her story with the vision of a "Retrospective" having its own ups and downs in a novel that takes victimisation as one of its themes. Nevertheless, Margaret Atwood seeing much more than the first person narrator does, allows her protagonist to turn to art-painting in this case which could have therapeutic effect. But unfortunately, instead of being cured by creativity, Elaine reverts in an obsessive manner, to her past; reliving an experience she would fain forget. Probably, she wants to have it reiterated that she is free of Cordelia but she feels "locked in" by a presence and she admits to herself, "I am not free, of Cordelia" (CE, p. 360). Indeed, Cordelia is that part of her identity which Elaine is trying to forego. Memories of past torture make her fragmented. "I am in fragments," she often says. Only when these old connections, which bind her to her particular identity in time, are severed, she is sure to feel whole.

Here, we are reminded of Nanda Kaul in Anita Desai's *Fire on the Mountain* and Bim in *Clear Light of Day*. Both wish to run away from past memories but both are tied down by them. In *Clear Light of Day*, Bim shudders at the thought of reliving her childhood and tells Tara that she would not like to revert to that time and undergo the torture; in *Cat's Eye*, Elaine shouts to a non-existent Cordelia, "I don't want to be nine years old forever" (CE, p. 400) because that child seems "younger, poorer, farther away, a shrunken, ignorant version of myself" (CE, p. 55). But Nanda, Bim and Elaine find their past inseparably linked with their lives. When it erodes their present, the three protagonists react according to their psychological exigencies: Nanda dies unable to bear the truth, Bim seeks solace in music and Elaine admits, as she flies away from Toronto, that once we shed our "old hates and grievances," like the two old women in the plane, we tend to be free of all prejudices and their scalding effect. "It's old light, and there's not much of it. But it's enough to see by" (CE, p. 421). She appears to have wiped out all malice towards Cordelia when she comments on the loss of companionship, "This is what I miss, Cordelia: not something that's gone, but something that will never happen. Two old women giggling over their tea" (CE, p. 421).

The author would have us believe in Elaine's march towards wholeness and health as she concludes the novel with an apparent healthy note:

> *Now it's full night, clear, moonless and filled with stars, which are not eternal as was once thought, which are not where we think they are. If they were sounds, they would be echoes, of something that happened millions of years ago: a word made of numbers. Echoes of light, shining out of the midst of nothing. It's old light, and there's not much of it. But it's enough to see by* (CE, p. 421).

Symbolically, the full, clear night with a star-studded sky can be interpreted as Elaine's conscience, which has rid itself of Cordelia and has gained her freedom. She has marched ahead, in time and only "echoes" are heard, not the real voice. If we consider this statement as an indication to a healthy attitude, then Elaine is a mentally sound woman who has got over her neurotic difficulties. But my contention is that Elaine's positive last statement is only an expression of her relief because she is leaving Toronto. Away from this town, she hopes to be at peace and immerse herself in her art as she has done earlier. This is an effort of the alienated self to ward off conflicts so as to protect her subjective values. In the following discussion I shall try to show as to why the status quo is maintained.

To cope which the hostile environment at Queen Mary Public school, Elaine develops a complex network of defenses. Because of her need to have "girl friends" and because she wants to earn their goodwill, she becomes humble, agreeable and pleasant. That she needs friends is clear from the list of "wants" on her eighth birthday: "I want some friends, friends who will be girls. Girl friends. I know that these exist, having read about them in books, but I've never had any girl friends because I've never been in one place long enough" (CE, p. 28). Thus, Elaine's primary solution is self-effacement. Her other strategies – withdrawal and mastery – subsidiary to it are not strong enough to come to the surface.

As the novel opens with Elaine's resolve to have a "Retrospective" of her paintings, we are able to see the three moves—withdrawal, mastery and compliance. But it is her compliant solution that rules her psyche and makes her miserable when she fails to stand up to her glorified image of a good, unselfish and devoted friend. Elaine acts in an aggressive manner only once when she "walks away" from Cordelia for which she suffers under scathing self-accusation. The thought that she has failed her friend gives a blow to her self-image. "I'm good at leaving. The trick is to close yourself off. Don't hear, don't see. Don't look back" (CE, p. 376). She blames herself thus and consequently wallows in self-contempt. "Whatever is happening to me is my own fault. I have done something wrong, something so huge I can't even see it, something that's drowning me. I am inadequate and stupid, without worth, I might as well be dead" (CE, p. 372). Since self-torture is "in part an inevitable by-product of self-hate" (NHG, p. 145), Elaine torments herself physically, as well as psychologically; physically by inflicting pain on herself and psychologically, by losing herself in all kinds of feelings like shutting herself off from others, wallowing in guilt-feelings, yearning for fading out in sleep and often in her death-wish as the ultimate extinction of self.

A question arises here: why does Elaine rebel and break away from Cordelia? It could be argued that she rebels out of desperation when the three girls reduce her to a "naught." She can no longer tolerate being abused and humiliated. Once she is able to disregard Cordelia's orders, she feels free of her. Not that Elaine has changed overnight into a bold young woman. She is afraid of Cordelia's anger and the sneers of others:

> *I am still a coward, still fearful; none of that has changed. But I turn and walk away from her. It's like stepping off a cliff, believing the air will hold you up. And it does. I see that I don't have to do what she says, and, for worse or better, I've never had to do what she says, I can do what I like (CE, p. 193).*

Cordelia becomes somewhat conciliatory after her daring act and Elaine gains confidence that she no longer needs them. "I am indifferent to them. There's something hard in me, crystalline, a kernel of glass" (CE, p. 193). Her mother, too, reinforces this attitude of self-assertion. She has always been advising her to stand up for herself. "Don't let them push you around. Don't be spineless. You have to have more backbone" (CE, p. 156). In Charlotte Brontë's *Jane Eyre*,[7] we confront an identical problem. Jane is abused, insulted and hurt despite her obedience and meekness. But when the attacks of the Reeds become unbearable, she rebels and fights back. Once she shows her strength, her tormentors change their attitude. Bessi approves of her "frank and fearless" behaviour and tells her that people will respect her better if she is bold and is able to stand for herself. In *Cat's Eye*, Elaine also sees a remarkable change in her friends' attitude towards her; they become "polite" but "distant". She even gains sufficient courage to answer Cordelia's "What do you think of me?" With "nothing much" (CE, p. 254), which though intended to be a joke, has a grain of truth in it. Thus, as a result of bitter experience, Elaine learns to resort to aggression when her compliance fails. Submission and revolt are two contradictory trends; they account for much of her conflicts in life.

Along with compliance and aggression, Elaine learns that withdrawal prevents problems and that resignation protects her from hostility. In childhood, she counters the sneers of Cordelia and others by learning to be quiet, "I've never said a lot anyway" (CE, p. 254), she confesses. She even becomes careless about her appearance as a grown-up young woman. Mrs Finestein reports to her mother, "she's letting herself go. Such a shame" (CE, p. 27). Elaine's mother is rightly concerned because this is an "alarming" sign. Horney feels that when a person withdraws from an active interest in his own growth, he is in the "danger of moving away also from the depths of his feelings" (NHG, p. 285). There are times in adult Elaine's life when she is pervaded with inertia:

> *I don't do anything else. I no longer go to the meetings of the women, because they make me feel worse. Jody phones and says we should get together, but I put her off. She would jolly me along, make bracing and positive suggestions I know I can't live up to. Then I would only feel more like a failure.*

> *I don't want to see anyone. I lie in the bedroom with the curtains drawn and nothingness washing over me like a sluggish wave. Whatever is happening to me is my own fault. I have done something wrong, something so huge I can't even see it, something that's drowning me. I am inadequate and stupid, without worth. I might as well be dead (CE, p. 372).*

Thus, she "removes herself from the inner battlefield," and becomes an "onlooker" on life (NHG, p. 260), without any will to participate in life. These measures relieve inner tensions to an extent.

Another method to run away from tension is the desire to be invisible which she expresses often. As a child, she imagines as if "my body is dissolving and I am being drawn up and up, like thinning mist, into a vast emptying space" (CE, p. 105). Invisibility gives one the power over others without exposing the self. Nanda Kaul in Anita Desai's *Fire on the Mountain* wants to be anonymous and her strong urge, is to "merge with the pine trees and be mistaken for one."[8] At another time her desire is to lie still, to be a "charred tree trunk." By withdrawing from the world of active life into a world of their own, these characters save their individuality from being altogether cramped and engulfed. When overpowered by Cordelia, Elaine thinks of being invisible:

> *I think about becoming invisible. I think about eating the deadly nightshade berries from the bushes beside the path. I think about drinking the Javex out of the skull-and-crossbones bottle in the laundry room, about jumping off the bridge, smashing down there like a pumpkin, half of an eye, half of a grin. I would come apart like that; I would be dead, like the dead people (CE, p. 155).*

In adult life, Elaine's wish to invisibility turns into death wish. Once she succumbs to it, she slashes her wrist to commit suicide.

Suicidal instinct works at two levels for Elaine: it gives her power over others, elevating her as a suffering martyr and it helps her ward off her self-hate. In the first case, it satisfies her self-effacing need. The fantasy of being looked after, with Jon by her side, Sarah nearby and the doctors hovering around her, she "felt white, drained of blood, cared for, purified. Peaceful" (CE, p. 374). Secondly, in addition to restoring her dwindling neurotic pride, it satisfies her masochistic longing for self-extinction. Horney sees "masochism" as arising out of the basic demands of self-effacing structure. It is not a "morbid phenomena" as seen by Freud and Karl Meninger. According to Horney, it arises out of a craving for love and it expresses itself through "demonstrative sufferings" in which a person feels ultimate triumph in "dying at the offender's doorstep" (NHG, p. 236). He or she develops feelings of all kind like losing himself/herself "in a sea of tears; in ecstatic feelings about nature; in wallowing in guilt-feelings… and often in his longing for death as the ultimate extinction of self" (NHG, pp. 240-41). Suffering has a special appeal for Elaine and it is a complex and compulsive phenomenon of her strategies.

Apart from fulfilling her need for love, suffering provides her the means to feel whole. As Elaine's feelings of fragmentation increase, she resorts to self-mutilation. She pulls the strips of flesh from her feet, nibbles her fingers and clips her nails till she feels the pain. This compulsion, developed in childhood, stays with her. Living with Jon years later, she falls on this habit. She recalls "When no one is around, I bite my fingers. I need to feel physical pain, to attach myself to daily life" (CE, p. 338). She chews her fingers to get the taste of blood, for blood is the "taste I remember." She confesses once that, she admires the wounds because "I know about the status conferred by" them (CE, p. 77). Obviously, these acts of self-mutilation and self-torture not only assuage her own self-accusation but also ward off the possible reproaches of others. Discussing the role of suffering for an expansive person, Horney believes that it is "his specific way of suppressing vindictiveness." Suffering provides Elaine with an overall alibi, both, for not actually making more of her life and for not achieving ambitious goal.

Elaine continues her suffering process by returning to her past and wallowing in self-pity as well as in guilt-feelings. Self-pity, for being a victim of Cordelia all through her life and guilt for having deserted Cordelia in the time of her need. "I am not sure I want to travel back into the past," she says, yet she reverts to it, blames Cordelia for torturing in childhood and for continuing to haunt her even after death. As Elaine remembers those past incidents, she suffers and reiterates "I don't want to remember. The past has become discontinuous, like stones skipped across water, like post cards" (CE, p. 302). Like Atwood's other heroines, Elaine, too, has difficulty with her past. In *Bodily Harm*, Rennie tries to put a lock on her past, the narrator of *Surfacing* fabricates her past, Joan of

Lady Oracle compartmentalises it and Elaine dreads hers. In the memory of the past, she catches "an image of myself, a dark blank, an image, a blank" (CE, p. 302). Elaine employs this strategy to actualise her idealised image of herself as a victim and significantly, its realisation depends on others, particularly on Cordelia who would:

> ...*alternate between kindness and malice, with periods of indifference; but now she's harsher, more relentless. It's as if she's driven by the urge to see how far she can go. She's backing me towards an edge, like the edge of a cliff: one-step back, another step, and I'll be over and falling (CE, p. 154).*

She is successful in projecting herself as her victimised, subdued self but both the narrator and the reader are confused at some point to know exactly which Cordelia is the culprit? "The one I have conjured up, the one with the roll-top boots and the turned-up collar, or the one before, or the one after? There is never only one, of anyone" (CE, p. 6). Obviously, Elaine, in recounting her life, has lost her 'self' and has become a split personality.

The split is between Elaine's two selves: effacing and aggressive. So far, we have seen her only as a victim of her peculiar circumstances and of Cordelia. But, there are indications of aggressive drives all through the narrative, which significantly point towards Elaine's duality, revealing her expansive self hidden underneath her subdued image. Elaine wants power. She needs to feel stronger. When power does not come easily, she seeks it vicariously in childhood through her marble "cat's eye." That the cat's eye has the power to protect her, is a secret, well guarded from Cordelia:

> *She doesn't know what power this cat's eye has, to protect me. Sometimes when I have it with me I can see the way it sees. I can see people moving like bright animated dolls, their mouths opening and closing but no real words coming out. I can look at their shapes and sizes, their colours, without feeling; anything else about them. I am alive in my eyes only (CE, p. 141).*

Later in life, she seeks power through her paintings. "I remember when I had ideas about eternal greatness, when I wanted to be Leonardo da Vinci" (CE, p. 225, emphasis added). With these qualifications in mind, Elaine could hardly be expected to toe the line set by others. She always likes to "think about things the others know nothing about" (CE, p. 141). She is, thus, a superior being who can master life. Since Cordelia with her overwhelming personality poses a danger to her image and reduces her to a "nothing", Elaine rebels and defies her tormentor. After her first act of rebellion, she gains confidence to handle her difficulties. She decides to streamline her life and take a course in Art. It becomes her "lifeline, my real life. Increasingly I begin to eliminate whatever does not fit in with it…" (CE, p. 276). Cordelia and others are eliminated at this stage.

However, Elaine cannot obliterate Cordelia from her consciousness. She becomes an integral part of her identity. Margaret Atwood uses mirror imagery to focus on Elaine's dual identity. When reflected in the mirror of Cordelia's sunglasses, Elaine appears "in duplicate and monochrome, and a great deal smaller than life size" (CE, p. 303). In psychoanalysis, the mirror metaphor has a symbolic significance as it functions of perceiving and being perceived. Lacan uses "mirror-phase" in which the child "perceives itself as other, an image, exterior to its own perceiving self, [which, thus] necessitates a splitting between the I which is perceived and the I which does the perceiving."[9] In Horneyan terminology, the mirror-imagery points towards intra-psychic conflict. As Stephen Ahern observes, "The fact that images of mirrors and reflections abound in *Cat's Eye*, and are a dominant motif in Elaine's paintings as well as in her inner life, underscores the possible symbolic significance of this psychoanalytic metaphor."[10] Mirror becomes the all-seeing eye:

> I become fascinated with the effects of glass, and of other light-reflecting surfaces. I study paintings in which there are pearls, crystals, mirrors and shiny details of brass. I spend a long time over Van Eyck's 'The Arnolfini Marriage', going over the inadequate colour print of it in my textbook with a magnifying glass; what fascinates me is not the two delicate, pallid, shoulderless hand-holding figures, but the pier-glass on the wall behind them, which reflects in its convex surface not only their backs but two other people who aren't in the main picture at all. These figures reflected in the mirror are slightly askew, as if a different law of gravity, a different arrangement of space, exists inside, locked in, sealed up in the glass as if in a paper-weight.

> *This round mirror is like an eye, a single eye that sees more than*
> *anyone else looking: over this mirror is written, "Johannes de*
> *Eyck fuit hic. 1434." It's disconcertingly like a washroom*
> *scribble, something you'd write with spray-paint on a wall (CE,*
> *p. 327).*

Elaine's childhood of negative self-image continues to have
the power over her "like a mirror that shows you only the ruined
half of your face" (CE, p. 410). Whenever she sees in the mirror,
she finds Cordelia standing near her, which disturbs her because,
as Stephen (Elaine's brother) observes, "Cordelia has a tendency
to exist" (CE, p. 242). Stephen's words suggest a relationship
based on dependency syndrome. This dependency brings her
needs into conflict. Although Cordelia's tendency to master is the
very characteristic which both attracts and repels Elaine, the
power Elaine has given Cordelia over herself threatens her
freedom. To avoid self-hate for being vulnerable and a victim,
Elaine exaggerates Cordelia's bullying nature, but it is actually the
"Iron-Lung" of her own need to submit which suffocates like
"some invisible leash" (CE, p. 93) around her neck. Elaine
develops a kind of love-hate relationship with Cordelia. In
moments of crisis she becomes Elaine's enemy, when the crisis is
over, she thinks of her as her friend. This love-hate relationship
accounts for much of her trouble in later life not only with regard
to herself and Cordelia but also in her human relationship. Just as
she has dual identity, she also has dual love relationships with Jon
and Joseph, simultaneously:

> *Two men are better than one, or at least they make me feel better.*
> *I am in love with both, I tell myself, and having two means that*
> *I don't have to make up my mind about either of them (CE, p.*
> *316).*

That Elaine stands on unsure grounds is illustrated by the
above lines. She is indecisive about the men in her life because as
she says, "my life is now multiple, and I am in fragments" (CE, p.
316). Flight from decision relieves her tension temporarily, but the
inner burden does not allow her the freedom. A continuous
conflict arises between her compliant and expansive selves. She
likes Cordelia because Cordelia is what Elaine would love to be –
powerful, masterly and triumphant; she hates Cordelia because
Cordelia by her domineering nature reduces her to "nothing." She

often indicts her, "Cordelia, I think you made me believe I was nothing" (CE, p. 199), to which she gets a careless reply "SO?" There is no answer to this. The trouble is, if Elaine accepts her self-effacing tendencies and identifies herself with goodness, meekness and helplessness, her expansive self will surface and it will chide her for being a willing victim, a spineless woman; if she becomes her aggressive triumphant self, then again conflict would be triggered off by her compliant nature for violating the norms of "good" behaviour. The easiest way of releasing tension is through passive externalisation. This shows in her "feeling accused by others, suspected or neglected, kept down, treated with contempt, abused, exploited or treated with outright cruelty" (NHG, p. 225). The scapegoat is Cordelia.

Because she can avoid self-hate only by avoiding responsibility for her loss of confidence, Elaine goes to a great deal of trouble to convince herself and the readers that she has been "driven" all her life, that she has always been "fragmented" and "unreal" and that she has been a "disembodied" self. The onus of responsibility thus shifts to others. In order to escape self-hate, she goes away from the suffocating milieu of Toronto and earns a name as a painter. She is in the limelight with her art exhibition getting good publicity and journalists coming to interview her. In spite of these attempts to escape self-hate and lead a normal life, Elaine is stuck down by half-truths, condemned to experience life in pieces.

Elaine's dreams manifest her inner turmoil. She dreams of the dead raven, the wooden bridge over the ravine falling apart, her mother not coming to her rescue when she is standing on the swaying bridge, the chokeberries turning into "deadly nightshade berries" which burst open and "blood runs over my hands" (CE, p. 145). Again, she dreams of being ashamed of her bare skin:

I dream I'm putting on my winter clothes, in Toronto, but my dress doesn't fit. I pull it on over my head and struggle to get my arms into the sleeves. I'm walking along the street and parts of my body are sticking out through the dress, parts of my bare skin. I am ashamed (CE, p. 145).

These dreams show the fear of self-hate and the approaching of self-alienation. Karen Horney corroborates the significance of dreams in understanding neurosis and in taking clue from them for the therapeutic process. The onslaught of self-hate and self-berating may appear in dreams even before the person is conscious of it. "He may present himself through the symbol of a cesspool, some loathsome creature... a gangster, a ridiculous clown. He may dream of houses with a pompous facade but inside as messy as a pigsty, of houses dilapidated beyond repair... of somebody making a fool of himself in public, etc" (NHG, p. 133). In another set of dreams, Elaine sees herself searching some lost treasure. Symbolically, it is her loss of identity that she is searching for. Horney elaborates the process thus:

> *In many ways the loss of identity can be expressed directly and succinctly. The dreamer may have lost his passport or when asked to identify himself was unable to do so. Or perhaps an old friend of his will appear in his dream looking quite different from the way he remembers him. Or he may look at a portrait but the picture frame encloses an empty canvas.*

> *Much more frequently the dreamer is not explicitly puzzled by the question of his identity but presents himself in terms of divergent symbols: different people, animals, plants or inanimate objects... the torturer and the tortured, the frightened child and the rattlesnake (NHG, p. 188).*

Elaine's dreams and her art expresses her unconsciousness to a large extent.

Just as her dreams expose her loss of identity, her paintings show her fragmentation. She has titled her works according to their themes. Significantly, they have eloquent themes—nature, figures from her past, her parents, brother, Mrs Finestein, Mr Banerji and others. Her self-portrait is entitled *Cat's Eye* and it eloquently expresses her fragmented self because in it she has painted only her half-face. The title expresses her need for power. While the painting reflects some of the elements of her past, it becomes a portrait of her inner turmoil. The foreground/background structures of her work with inner/outer split and half face/full face focus displays the inner duality of Elaine. That Cordelia is only the half-self of Elaine is clear from the painting depicting Cordelia, and named *Half A Face*.

Elaine makes us believe that she is a displaced person who has lost touch with her inner self, but we realise that she is not a demented woman. There are times when she seems to be in touch with the centre. It is not contended here that Elaine achieves wholeness or that she has found a final resolution to her quest for identity. On the contrary, she tosses like a shuttle-cock between her past and present, blurring the traces of self-understanding, if any. She builds up the defences and becomes acutely aware of the world around her, and as Stephen Ahern points out "her psychological development is arrested in a kind of atemporal stasis."[11] But, despite being trapped, she saves herself from being a disembodied being. She comes to terms with some of the demons of her past. In rare moments of illumination, Elaine understands human limitations. If Mrs Smeath has been harsh on her, it was not because she was bad, it was because she was trapped in "a small town thread bare decency" and was herself a "displaced person" (CE, p. 405). Elaine realises that malice and vengeance do not allow one to see clearly, "an eye for an eye leads only to more blindness" (CE, p. 405). One must have a broader vision without being encumbered by prejudices.

Similarly, she understands Cordelia's position too. Cordelia was isolated at her home where there was silence, lack of love and understanding. She took her vengeance on her friends at school by bossing over them. The sufferer was Cordelia, her friends suffered only by implication. An adult Elaine asserts that she is not afraid of Cordelia but she is afraid of *being* Cordelia. "I'm not afraid of seeing Cordelia. I'm afraid of being Cordelia. Because in some way we changed places, and I've forgotten when" (CE, p. 227). Elaine would not like to merge her identity with Cordelia, because Cordelia is, after all, not the stronger of the two. Elaine forgives Cordelia as she sees clearly that the flaws for which she suffered guilt were not hers at all:

> *I know she's looking at me, the lopsided mouth smiling a little, the face closed and defiant. There is the same shame, the sick feeling in my body, the same knowledge of my wrongness, awkwardness, weakness; the same wish to be loved; the same loneliness; the same fear. But these are not my own emotions any more. They are Cordelia's; as they always were (CE, p. 419).*

In her forgiveness lies her freedom. This does not mean that she has resolved her crisis, nor does this suggest that she goes away from Toronto cured of her self-alienation. The

"Retrospective" has given her the scope to transfer her vision from being "ego-centered" to "problem-centered."[12] Significantly, the last chapter is named *Bridge*, which suggests the ability to join two parallel lines or banks. Standing on the bridge, Elaine recasts her past once again. She remembers the day she fell into water and froze to death; the epiphanic moment when Virgin Mary had rescued her. That time is past now. A mature, adult Elaine hears no voice, sees no vision. "There was only darkness and silence. Nobody and nothing" (CE, p. 418). This sense of "nothingness" is devoid of all bitterness. It fills her with relief. She accepts the landscape as it is. "The bridge is only a bridge, the river a river, the sky is a sky" (CE, p. 419). It is impersonal, no longer subjective. The landscape is both "empty" and "not empty" like her. She reconstructs Cordelia's weakness and her strength; forgives her, as indicated by the line "the snow in my eyes withdraws like smoke" (CE, p. 419) and Elaine flies away from the disturbing milieu of Toronto. The I/Thou dichotomy still holds good in Elaine's psyche; as the plane flies westward, she looks at the sinking sun. It appears "a murderous, vulgar, unpaintable and glorious display of red and purple and orange" (CE, p. 420). This is suggestive of a future, bright but "murderous." Behind her, "The ordinary night rolls forward," it is indicative of the past, which she has tried to obliterate. Elaine comprehends the human weakness of Mrs Smeath, Cordelia, Jon and Josef. She also understands the futility of judging others because every human being is entrapped by his or her situation. She has taken her revenge on them by painting them as she saw them: mean Mrs Smeath, half-faced Cordelia, uncertain Mr Banerji and helpless Stephen. Art has released her tension, and now she no longer wishes to judge people.

References

1. Margaret Laurence, *The Stone Angel* (Toronto: Seal Books, 1984).

2. Judith Thurman, "When You Wish Upon a Star," *The New Yorker* (29 May 1989), pp 108-10.

3. Martha Sharpe, "Margaret Atwood and Julia Kristeva: Space-Time, the Dissident Woman Artist, and the Pursuit of Female Solidarity in *Cat's Eye.*" *Essays on Canadian writing*. No. 50 (Fall 1993), p. 175.

4. Martha Sharpe, p. 174.

5. Earl G.Ingersoll, "Waltzing Again." in *Margaret Atwood: Conversations*, ed. Earl G. Ingersoll (Ontario: Ontario Review Press, 1990), p. 235.

6. R. D. Lane, "Cordelia' s "Nothing": The Character of Cordelia and Margaret Atwood's *Cat's Eye."* *Essays on Canadian Writing*, No. 48 (Winter 1992-93), p. 78.

7. Charlotte Brontë, *Jane Eyre* (New Delhi: Atlantic Publishers, 1974).

8. Anita Desai, *Fire on the Mountain* (New Delhi: Allied, 1977), p. 4.

9. Catherine Belsey, *Critical Practice* (London: Routledge, 1989), p. 64.

10. Stephen Ahern, "Meat Like You Like It: The Production of Identity in Atwood's *"Cat's Eye."* *Canadian Literature.* No. 137 (Summer 1993), p. 14.

11. Stephen Ahern, 'Meat Like You Like It,' p. 8.

12. Richard J. Lowry, *A. H. Maslow: An Intellectual Portrait* (California: Books/Cole Publishing Company, 1973), p. 47.

CHAPTER 8

Conclusion

The preceding discussion points to a significant fact that Margaret Atwood is a great analyst of the human mind and profound interpreter of life. She has presented a myriad of realistic portraits. When we probe her characters' psychology, we see them as human beings with their weaknesses and potentialities. They are caught in the web of their own compulsions. When they are understood psychoanalytically we begin to visualise their ambitions, disappointments and loneliness as real. Margaret Atwood's rendering of their neurotic behaviour, their interaction and their solutions help us to fathom human nature and to grasp the subjective inner reality intuitively.

Atwood does not create characters independent of social or political issues or realism. She concentrates on the psychological intricacies of the behaviour of her protagonists who while living in society and facing the common problems struggle to find the meaning in life. Atwood believes that "fiction is one of the few forms left through which we may examine our society not in its particular but in its typical aspects."[1] Her characters also show the concern of the modern man with the external human situation. Her narrative skill with its satiric or ironic content, its spontaneity and freshness indicates her rich creative faculty. Her characters hold the attention of readers when they tell their tales and embody their creator's vision of life.

Atwood's protagonists whether men or women, are living individuals, not case studies. They are interested in life with its hopes and disappointments. Their trouble is that they, at times, take a wrong path and perpetuate their neurosis. The narrator of *Surfacing* becomes divided self; the narrator of *Lady Oracle* is the multiple self; Elaine is the fragmented self of her twin self; Rennie suffers from fractured identity and Marian becomes the mirrored self of Peter. These characters are not heroes or heroines far above human weaknesses; nor do they have mythical dimensions. They are ordinary human beings with normal limitations. The strength of her fiction lies in the mimetic presentation of her experiences. Atwood's characters are moved by the aesthetic of existence. In studying works of art in the light of Horneyan psychology we do not detach characters from their aesthetic and thematic patterns. From this point of view a majority of her characters, for example, narrators of *Lady Oracle* and *Surfacing*, Lesje and Rennie live either in illusions by retreating into fabrications and fantasy or are unwilling to face reality. Then there are characters who compromise with life: Elizabeth and Marian. Although her characters have their conflicts, they manage to transcend their personal problems. Elaine affirms life; she accepts her past and looks forward to future. In Rennie and Elizabeth, there is a resolution to affirm life. Elaine is able to separate life from illusions. Her art liberates her. The growing urge for self-discovery of Atwood's characters shows their growth potential. Marian resolves not to become a consummable commodity but a person who can make choices about her life. The narrator of *Surfacing* endeavours to link herself with the past by discovering her father and accepting her complicity in abortion. She displays her resolve and strength to face life. *Lady Oracle's* protagonist though a fantasiser by nature does not give up the human hope of being a good wife to Arthur. She discovers her weaknesses and ultimately her essential nature. Elizabeth is torn when she loses her lover Chris and when her husband leaves her for a younger woman but she discovers her freedom and strength to accept life's responsibility to raise two children "single, alone." Lesje who has been evading reality of the lived present, also decides to opt for life instead of being co-opted. Her decision to stop using the pills and bear Nate's child indicates her new-found will to act. Rennie sees life with open eyes in the prison and resolves to be a reporter.

Atwood analyses the inner working of the mind of her characters. She displays the psyche of a woman who has to abort her child against her wishes in *Surfacing*. In *Surfacing* and *Bodily Harm* she probes the essential loneliness of a woman. Elizabeth is alone when Chris commits suicide and her husband Nate leaves her. Marian's basic problem is how to exist in a consumer society and maintain her individuality. Atwood's primary concern in all her works is not how one gets along with others but with oneself. Elaine's fears are psychological. She has taken her revenge, she walked on Caroline in her time of need but instead of feeling triumphant, Elaine feels unhappy with her callous self. Atwood presents action through the minds of these people shifting their mental time backward and forward. Virginia Woolf calls it the "tunnelling process" by which she recasts the past.

A scrutiny of Atwood's art shows that the novelist is growth-oriented, though she, in her article on W. D. Valgardson's fiction, refutes the idea of "growth" and "development" of a writer. She says that "writers are not radish" that they can grow. "If you look at what most writers actually do," she says, "it resembles a theme with variations, more than it does the popular notion of growth. Writers' universe may become more elaborate, but they do not necessarily become essentially different."[2] The development from her first heroine Marian to her latest creation Elaine is the story of evolution towards self-realisation. Some of her characters are independent of spirits. Being dissatisfied with routine world they break away from ordinary life patterns to realise that human ties cannot be substituted. By thus running away from the routine of their boring world, they seek some kind of fulfilment in their lonely existence and are drawn to their environment to realise that individual freedom must create some kind of relatedness or a new kind of relationship. Rennie who has run away to the Caribbean islands, reaches out to Lora whom she initially hated. Lesje who seeks fulfilment in a world of dinosaurs, make a move towards Nate. Elizabeth holds the hands of her dying aunt. They realise that escape, or showing apathy or indifference are not the answers to life's problems. They find meaning in their lives in their relatedness. They respond to human situation naturally rather than reacting neurotically.

The study reveals that Marian, Rennie and Joan Foster are very sensitive and are pitted against their insensitive partners. In the case of Lesje, her partner is too sensitive to hurt anyone, either Lesje or Elizabeth. Then there are Elaine and Elizabeth who are themselves too insensitive to their partners. Under the first category falls Marian, narrator of *Surfacing*, Joan Foster and Rennie. They are compliant. They value love and sex beyond everything in the world. When lover/fiancé/husband does not stand up to their expectations, they turn self-destructive in their fits of self-hate. The morbid dependency of Rennie and the narrator of *Surfacing* and the compliance of *Lady Oracle* are the outcome of their social or familial environment. We realise later that their alienation and troubles are not due to disturbances in their relationships, but they are the results of their own inner conflicts. There are cases of neurosis: the narrator of *Surfacing*, though she does not drown herself in the lake, Joan Foster fakes suicide, Elizabeth goes temporarily astray. Chris's suicide works havoc on her psyche. The fear of losing Nate's love disturbs her. Lesje's death wish owes to the failure of self-effacing solution. Joan Foster's self-hate tears her apart. In the case of Rennie, the destructive effect of self-alienation is almost neurotic.

Though Atwood's characters appear morbid, they are not insane. We may not term them self-actualising, but, we cannot disregard their brief moments of self-discovery. Their affirmation gives us hope that they can be spontaneous in their feelings if they do not oscillate between one neurotic solution to another. We find clarity of perception in Elaine. Her vision acquires authenticity. She finds her lost twin self in Cordelia and achieves self-realisation. Elizabeth has also an affirming faith in life. Lesje shows the same affirmation when she opts for life and is resolved to create. The narrator of *Lady Oracle* and Rennie reveal self-strength and show a tendency to emerge out of their self-alienation, insecurity and anxiety, and opt for life. Joan Foster is ready to nurse the man whom she has hit on the nose. Thus, these characters, in the process of individuation, reveal strength and gain a kind of integration and closeness. Elizabeth, Lesje and Rennie compromise with life after recognising their self. In *Surfacing* and *Lady Oracle*, the protagonists accept to fight the battle of life. After much agony they recover themselves. The presentation of struggle of such individuals is Atwood's forte.

Atwood, by portraying a variety of characters, plumbs deep into the secret recesses of the human psyche, which eludes comprehension. Except for Nate, her protagonists are women. She understands their mental, moral, aesthetic domains and struggles. The totality of human experience imports a deep perspective to her fiction. Her characters are questers. Marian's endeavour is to attain humanity and a human identity in a consumer society which literally and metaphorically traps her. Marian's quest is for a meaningful identity, at socio-political level, her quest is to become neither a man nor a machine but a woman with an absolute as against a relatively defined identity. The narrator of *Surfacing* is searching her roots, Joan of *Lady Oracle* is finding out what she has become after multiplying her selves. Elizabeth is trying to seek whether she can become a "good mother" after wrecking matrimony with fangs of infidelity and her neurotic needs. Rennie is probing through the Caribbean islands on how to get back to life and reporting. Elaine goes to her hometown in search of her lost childhood. Some come out successful, others have reached the banks. In projecting life, Atwood has displayed excellent ability of narrative art. It is art-painting in the case of Elaine and writing in the case of the narrator of *Lady Oracle* that restore their faith in life. It is life seen in itself in the light of sordidness which intensifies Rennie's wish to explore the outer and physical world. Lesje's fantasising ends when it clashes with reality. Her comprehension of everyday reality opens her up to the joys of living personal relationships. She and Rennie experience emotional and social wholeness by experiencing a relationship with human life.

Atwood's characters have their psychological compulsions and fears. They go through the hell of self-condemnation. They run from themselves, some reach the edge. But all of them come out of this alienation. In *The Edible Woman*, Marian bakes a cake and takes a decision. In *Surfacing*, the narrator visualises herself coming to Joe. Something in them, some force or drive, momentary collision with reality and illusion bring them back to life. Rennie wills herself to hold Lora's hand and affirms her will to participate in the deep processes of human intercourse. She regains her identity as a whole human being as against her earlier incomplete self.

In sum, the aesthetic pleasure in Margaret Atwood is derived from a perfect correlation between technique, art and content. Her technique reinforces her artistic vision of life. Technique, according to Mark Schorer, is the means an author has "of discovering, exploring, developing his subject, of conveying its meaning and finally evaluating it."[3] Atwood's technique covers the entire range of her experience on which she paints her subject matter. It gains in meaning and completeness of expression through the use of narrative devices, such as symbols, dreams, linguistic methods and plot structure to give shape to her thematic contents. Thus her main concern, that of portraying the troubled psyche, is perfectly geared to depict the conflicts, dependence, aggression, neurotic pride, withdrawal and alienation of her protagonists. The conflict in her characters, their defence mechanism and their psychic life, all are objectified in the novels in a disguised form. Atwood's vision displays a kind of formal unity. She creates a fictive world in which her characters live, struggle with life and try to come to grips with the lived reality. This world is as real as the world we inhabit and the tensions of the personages living in this world are also as real. It is a triumph of Atwood's art as a novelist that she weaves the rich experience of life with her rich artistic material and produces mimetic pictures. The characters are highly distinctive in their motivations, conflicts, manners and methods, and lend depth to her art.

References

1. Margaret Atwood, *Second Words*: Selected Critical Prose (Toronto: Anansi, 1982), p. 346.

2. Quoted by Sherill E. Grace, "Articulating the 'Space Between': Atwood's Untold stories and French Beginnings," p. 4.

3. Mark Schorer, "Technique as Discovery," in *The Theory of the Novel*, ed. Philip Stevick (New York: The Free Press, 1967), p. 66.

Bibliography

Primary Sources

Atwood, Margaret. *Alias Grace*. Toronto: McClelland & Stewart, 1996.

——. *The Blind Assassin*. New York: Anchor Books, 2000.

——. *Bodily Harm*. New York: Bantam Books, 1983.

——. *Cat's Eye*. London: Virago Press, 1990.

——. *The Edible Woman*. Toronto: The Canadian Publishers, 1973.

——. *The Handmaid's Tale*. Boston: Houghton Muffin Company, 1986.

——. *Lady Oracle*. Toronto: The Canadian Publishers, 1976.

——. *Life Before Man*. New York: Ballantine Books, 1987.

——. *Oryx and Crake*. New York: Nan A. Talese Doubleday, 2003.

——. *Surfacing*. London: Virago Press, 1979.

——. "Face To Face." Woodcock, A Place to Stand on 20-27.

——. Foreword to *Ambivalence: Studies in Canadian Literature*. Ed. Om P. Juneja and Chandra Mohan. New Delhi: Allied, 1990.

——. Introduction to *The New Oxford Book of Canadian Verse*. Ed. Atwood. Don Mills: Oxford University Press, 1982, XXVII-XXXIX.

——. *The Journals of Susanna Moodie*. Toronto: Oxford University Press, 1970.

——. *Second Words: Selected Critical Prose*. Toronto: Anansi, 1982.

——. *Survival: A Thematic Guide to Canadian Literature*. Toronto: Anansi, 1972.

——. "Surviving the Critics: Mathews and Misrepresentation." *This Magazine is About Schools*, no. 7 (May-June 1973): 29-33.

——. *You Are Happy*. Toronto: Oxford University Press, 1974.

Secondary Sources

Abdi, Urooj. *Death Anxiety*. New Delhi: Radha Publication, 1990.

Adamson, Arthur. "Identity through Metaphor: An Approach to the question of Regionalism in Canadian Literature." *Studies in Canadian Literature* 5.1 (Spring 1980): 83-99.

Ahern, Stephen. "Meat Like You Like It: The Production of Identity in Atwood's 'Cat's Eye'." *Canadian Literature*, no. 137 (Summer 1993): 8-14.

Anant, S. S. "Conflict Resolution Through Belongingness." *Manas* 26, nos. 1-2 (1979).

Aranson, David, Dennis Cooley and Robert Enright. "Interview with Eli Mandel, March 16/78." *Essays on Canadian Writing* 18-19, (Summer-Fall 1980): 70-89.

Arnold, Matthew. *Culture and Anarchy*. Ed. J. Dover Wilson. Cambridge: University Press, 1971.

Atwood, Margaret. "Canadian-American Relations: Surviving The Eighties." *Glimpses of Canadian Literature*. Eds. C D. Narasimhaiah, C. N. Srinath and Wendy Keitner. Mysore: Dhvanyaloka Publication, 1985. 235-236.

Ballstadt, Carl. Ed. *The Search for English-Canadian Literature: An Anthology of Critical Articles from the Nineteenth and Early Twentieth Centuries*. Toronto and Buffalo: University of Toronto Press, 1975.

Beauvoir, Simone de. *The Second Sex*. Trans. and ed. H. M. Parshley. London: Penguin Books, 1949.

Belsey, Catherine. *Critical Practice*. London: Routledge, 1989.

Beran, Carol. *Living over the Abyss: Margaret Atwood's 'Life before Man'*. Toronto: ECW, 1994.

Birbalsingh, Frank. "National Identity and the Canadian Novel." *Journal of Canadian Fiction* 1.1 (Winter 1972): 56-59.

Bouson, J. Brooks. *Brutal Choreographies: Oppositional Strategies and Narrative Design in the Novels of Margaret Atwood*. Amherst: University of Massachusetts Press, 1993.

Broege, Valerie. "Margaret Atwood's Americans and Canadians." *Essays on Canadian Writing* 22 (Summer 1981): 111-135.

Bromberg, Pamela S. "The Two Faces of the Mirror." *Margaret Atwood: Vision and Forms*. Southern Illinois: Southern Illinois University Press, 1988.

Brontë, Charlotte. *Jane Eyre*. New Delhi: Atlantic Publishers, 1974.

Brown, E. K. "The Problem of a Canadian Literature." *On Canadian Poetry*. Toronto: The Ryerson Press, 1943. Rpt. in Brown, *Responses and Evaluations*. 1-23.

——. *Responses and Evaluations: Essays on Canada*. Ed. David Staines. Toronto: McClelland and Stewart, 1977.

Brown, Russell M. "Atwood's Sacred Wells." *Essays on Canadian Writing* 17 (Spring 1980): 5-43.

Brydon, Diana. "New Approaches to the New Literatures in English: Are we in Danger of Incorporating Disparity?" *A Shaping of Connections: Commonwealth Literature Studies – Then and Now. Essays in Honour of A. N. Jeffares*. Eds. Hena Maes-Jelinek, Kristen Holst Petersen and Anna Rutherford. Sidney/Mundelstrup/Coventry: Dangaroo Press, 1989. 89-99.

Cambell, Josie P. "The Woman as Hero in Margaret Atwood's '*Surfacing*'." *Post-War Canadian Fiction*. Ed. John Wortley. Winnipeg: University of Manitoba Press, 1978.

Cameron, Elspeth. *Atwood-The Edible Woman: Notes*. Coles Notes. Toronto: Coles, 1983.

Campbell, Joseph. *The Hero with a Thousand Faces*. 1949; rpt. Princeton: Princeton University Press, 1973.

Caplan, P. *Barriers Between Women*. Jamaica, New York: Spectrum Publications, 1981.

Carrington, Ildiko De Papp. *Margaret Atwood and Her Works*. Toronto: ECW, 1985. Coles Editorial Board. *Atwood-Surfacing: Notes*. Coles Notes. Toronto: Coles, 1982.

Child, Philip. "Fiction." *Canadian Literature Today. A Series of Broadcasts sponsored by The Canadian Broadcasting Corporation*. Toronto: University of Toronto Press, 1938. 31-36.

Chopin, Kate. *The Awakening*. New York: The Modern Library, 1981.

Christ, Carol P. "Margaret Atwood: The Surfacing of Women's Spiritual Quest and Vision." *Signs: A Journal of Women in Culture and Society* 2, no. 2 (Winter 1976): 316-30.

Cooper, John A. "Should our Literature Be Canadian?" *Canadian Magazine* VIII (April 1897): 544-45. Rpt. in Ballastadt, 107-10.

Cude, Wilfred. "Bravo Mothball! An Essay on '*Lady Oracle*'," in *The Canadian Novel: Here and Now*. Ed. John Moss. Toronto: Anansi, 1978, p. 48.

Davey, Frank. *Margaret Atwood: A Feminist Poetics*. Vancouver: Talonbooks, 1984.

———. *Reading Canadian Reading*. Winnipeg, Manitoba: Canada Turnstone Press, 1988.

———. *Surviving The Paraphrase: Eleven Essays on Canadian Literature*. Winnipeg: Turnstone Press, 1983.

———. *From There to Here; A Guide to English Literature Since 1960 Our Nature-Our Voices*. Vol. II. 1974. Erin, Ontario: P. Porcepic, 1975.

———. "Atwood Walking Backwards." *Open Letter* 2nd ser. 5 (Summer 1973): 74-85.

Davidson, Arnold E. and Cathy N. *The Art of Margaret Atwood: Essays in Criticism*. Toronto: Anansi, 1981.

Davis, Robertson. "The Canada of Myth and Reality." *One Half of Robertson Davies*. Toronto: Macmillan, 1977. Rpt. in *Canadian Literature in the 70's*. Eds. Paul Denham and Mary Jane Edwards. Toronto: Holt, Rinehart and Winston, 1980. 1-17.

Desai, Anita. *Bye-Bye, Black Bird*. New Delhi: Orient Paperbacks, 1971.

———. *Clear Light of the Day*. New Delhi: Allied, 1977.

———. *Cry, the Peacock*. New Delhi: Hind Pocket Books, 1963.

———. *Fire on the Mountain*. New Delhi: Allied, 1977.

———. *Voices in the City*. New Delhi: Orient Paperbacks, 1968.

Deshpande, Shashi. *The Binding Vine*. New Delhi: Penguin India, 1993.

———. *The Dark Holds No Terror*. New Delhi: Penguin India, 1980.

Dhar, T. N. "First Person Singular: The Raised Feminine Consciousness in Atwood's '*The Edible Woman*'." *Feminism and Recent Fiction in English*. Ed. Sushila Singh. New Delhi: Prestige, 1991.

Djwa, Sandra. "The Canadian Forum: Literary Catalyst." *Studies in Canadian Literature* 1.1 (Winter 1976): 7-25.

Dopp, Jamie. "Subject-Position As Victim Position In *The Handmaid's Tale.*" *Studies in Canadian Literature* 19, no. 1(1994).

Eldredge, Patricia Reid. "Karen Horney and Clarissa: The Tragedy of Neurotic Pride." *American Journal of Psychoanalysis* 42 (1982): 51-59.

Fabre, Michel. "From *'The Stone Angel to The Diviners'*: An Interview with Margaret Laurence." *A Place to Stand On.* Ed. Woodcock. 193-209.

Fee, Margery. "The Fat Lady Dances: Margaret Atwood's *'Lady Oracle'.*" Toronto: ECW, 1993.

Fenwick, Julie. "The Silence of the Mermaid: *Lady Oracle* and *Anne of Green Gables.*" *Essays on Canadian Writing*, no. 47 (Fall 1992): 51-52.

Ferres, John. "Forum Survival to Affirmation: New Perspectives in Canadian Literary Criticism." *American Review of Canadian Studies* 3.1 (Spring 1973): 123-33.

Firestone, Shulamith. *The Dialectic of Sex: The Case For Feminist Revolution.* New York: William Morow, 1970.

Fraser, Wayne. *The Dominion of Women.* New York: Greenwood Press, 1991.

Fromm, Erich and Ramon Xirau, Eds. *The Nature of Man.* New York: Macmillan, 1968.

Fromm, Erich. *Escape from Freedom.* New York: Rinehart, 1941.

———. *Man For Himself: An Inquiry into the Psychology of Ethics.* Great Britain: Routledge and Kegan Paul Ltd., 1949.

———. *Psychoanalysis and Religion.* New Haven: Yale University Press, 1950.

———. *The Anatomy of Human Destructiveness.* New York: Holt, Rinehart and Winston, 1973.

———. *The Art of Loving.* 1957; rpt. London: Unwin Paperbacks, 1976.

———. *The Dogma of Christ and Other Essays on Religion, Psychology and Culture.* New York: Holt, Rinehart and Winston, 1963.

———. *The Fear of Freedom.* 1942; rpt. London: Routledge and Kegan Paul, 1960.

———. *The Forgotton Language: An Introduction to the Understanding of Dreams, Fairy Tales and Myths.* New York: Rinehart and Winston, 1951.

Fromm, Erich. *The Heart of Man, Its Genius for Good and Evil*. New York: Harper and Row, 1964.

———. *The Sane Society*. 1956; rpt. London: Routledge and Kegan Paul, 1963.

———. *To Have or to Be?* New York: Harper and Row, 1976.

Frye, Northrop. Conclusion. *Literary History of Canada: Canadian Literature in English*. Ed. Carl F. Klinck et al. 1st ed. 3 Vols. Toronto; University of Toronto Press, 1965. Rpt. in Frye Bush Garden, 213-51.

———. *Divisions on a Ground: Essays on Canadian Culture*. Ed. James Polk. Toronto: Anansi, 1982.

———. *The Bush Garden: Essays on the Canadian Imagination*. Toronto: Anansi, 1971.

———. Conclusion [Revised]. Klinck 3: 318-32.

Garrett-Petts, W. F. "Reading, Writing and the Post-Modern Condition: Interpreting Atwood's '*The Handmaid's Tale*'." *Open Letter* 7th ser. 1 (Spring 1988): 74-92.

Garrison, Dee. "Karen Horney and Feminism." *Signs: Journal of Women in Culture and Society* 6 (1981): 672-91.

Gibson, Graeme. "Margaret Atwood." *Eleven Canadian Novelists*. Toronto: Anansi, 1973. 1-31.

Givner, Jessie. "Names and Signatures in Margaret Atwood's '*Cat's Eye*' and '*The Handmaid's Tale*'." *Canadian Literature*, no. 133 (Summer 1992).

Godard, Barbara. "A Portrait with Three Faces: The New Woman in Fiction by Canadian Women, 1880-1920." *Glimpses of Canadian Literature*. Eds. C. D. Narasimhaiah, C. N. Srinath and Wendy Keitner. Mysore: Dhvanyaloka Publication, 1985. 72-92.

Goetsch, Paul. "Margaret Atwood's '*Life Before Man*' as a Novel of Manners." *Gaining Ground: European Critics on Canadian Literature*. Eds. Robert Kroetsch and Reingard M. Nischik. Edmonton: Newest Press, 1985. 137-49.

Gomez, Christine. "From Being an Unaware Victim to Becoming a Creative Non-Victim: A Study of Two Novels of Margaret Atwood." *Perspectives on Canadian Fiction*. Ed. Sudhakar Pandey. New Delhi: Prestige Books, 1994.

Grace, Sherill E. *Violent Duality; A Study of Margaret Atwood.* Montreal: Vehicule Press, 1980.

———. "Articulating the 'Space Between': Atwood's Untold Stories and Fresh Beginnings." Grace and Weir 1-16.

Grace, Sherrill E. and Lorraine Weir, Eds. *Margaret Atwood: Language, Text And System.* Vancouver: University of British Columbia Press, 1983.

Grant, George. *Lament for a Nation: The Defeat of Canadian Nationalism.* 1965; rpt. Toronto/Montreal: McClelland and Stewart, 1971.

Guedon, Marie Francoise. "Surfacing: Amerindian Themes and Shamanism." Grace and Weir 91-111.

Harris, Thomas A. *I'm OK-You' re OK.* New York: Avon Books, 1967.

Harrison, Dick. "The Search for an Authentic Voice in Canadian Literature." *Ambivalence: Studies in Canadian Literature.* Eds. Om P. Juneja and Chandra Mohan. New Delhi: Allied, 1990. 67-80.

Harvey, W. J. *Character and the Novel.* New York: Ithaca, 1965.

Hengen, Shannon. *Margaret Atwood's Power: Mirrors, Reflections And Images in Select Fiction And Poetry.* Toronto: Second Story Press, 1993.

Horney, Karen. "The Paucity of Inner Experiences." *American Journal of Psychoanalysis* 12 (1952): 3-9. Rpt. in Kelman, 1964, pp. 47-64 and Rubins, 1972, pp. 97-103.

———. "The Value of Vindictiveness." *American Journal of Psychoanalysis* 8 (1948): 3-12. Rpt. in Kelman, 1965, pp. 27-51.

———. Ed. *Are You Considering Psychoanalysis?* New York: Norton, 1946.

———. *Feminine Psychology.* Ed. Harold Kalman. New York: Norton, 1967.

———. *New Ways in Psychoanalysis.* New York: Norton, 1939.

———. *Our Inner Conflicts: A Constructive Theory of Neurosis.* New York: Norton, 1945.

———. *Self-Analysis.* New York: Norton, 1942.

———. *The Adolescent Diaries of Karen Horney.* New York: Basic Books, 1980.

Horney, Karen. *The Neurotic Personality of Our Time.* New York: Norton, 1937.

———. *Neurosis and Human Growth: The Struggle Toward Self-Realization.* 1951; rpt. London: Routledge and Kegan Paul, 1965.

Howells, Coral Ann. *Margaret Atwood.* New York: St. Martin's Press, 1996.

———. *York Notes on The Handmaid's Tale.* Harlow, Essex: Longman, 1993.

Hutcheon, Linda. "From Poetic to Narrative Structures: The Novels of Margaret Atwood." *Margaret Atwood: Language, Text And System,* Eds. Sherril E. Grace and Lorraine Weir. Vancouver: University of British Columbia Press, 1983.

———. *The Canadian Postmodern: A Study of Contemporary English-Canadian Fiction.* Toronto: Oxford University Press, 1988.

Ingersoll, Earl G. "Waltzing Again." *Margaret Atwood: Conversations.* Ed. Earl G. Ingersoll. Ontario: Ontario Review Press, 1990.

———. Ed. *Margaret Atwood: Conversations.* Princeton, New Jersey: Ontario Review Press, 1990.

Irvine, Lorna. *Collecting Clues: Margaret Atwood's Bodily Harm.* Toronto: ECW, 1994.

———. *Collecting Clues: Margaret Atwood's 'Bodily Harm'.* ECW Press, Toronto, 1993, McCombs, Judith, Editor. *Critical Essays On Margaret Atwood.* G. K. Hall & Co., Boston, 1988.

Jhabvala, Ruth. *Heat and Dust.* London: Futura Macdonald and Co., 1976.

Kaur, Iqbal. *Margaret Atwood's Surfacing: A Critical Study.* Chandigarh: Arun Publishing House, 1994.

Keith, W. J. *Introducing Margaret Atwood's The Edible Woman: A Reader's Guide.*

Klapp, Orrin E. *Collective Search for Identity.* New York: Holt, Rinehart and Winston, 1969.

Klinck, Carl F., et al Eds. *Literary History of Canada: Canadian Literature in English.* 1965. 2nd ed-3 vols. Toronto and Buffalo: University of Toronto Press, 1976.

Kohut, H. *The Analysis of the Self.* New York: International Universities Press, 1971.

Kolodny, Annette. "Margaret Atwood And the Politics of Narrative." *Studies on Canadian Literature.* Ed. Arnold E. Davidson. New York: The Modern Language Association of America, 1990.

Krishnamurti, J. *Beyond Violence.* London: Victor Gollancz, 1973.

Kroetsch, Robert. "Contemporary Standards in the Canadian Novel." Steele 9-19.

Laing, R. D. *The Divided Self. An Existential Study in Sanity and Madness.* London: Penguin, 1969.

Lane, R. D. "Cordelia's 'Nothing': The Character of Cordelia and Margaret Atwood's 'Cat's Eye'." *Essays on Canadian Writing,* no. 48 (Winter 1992-93).

Laurence, Margaret. *The Diviners.* Toronto: Anansi, 1974.

———. *A Jest of God.* Toronto: Seal Books, 1978.

———. *The Fire-Dwellers.* Toronto: Seal Books, 1983.

———. *The Stone Angel.* Toronto: Seal Books, 1984.

Lowry, Richard J. *A.H. Maslow: An Intellectual Portrait.* California: Books/Cole Publishing Company, 1973.

MacLulich, T. D. "The Survival Shoot-out." *Essays on Canadian Writing* 1 (Winter 1974): 14-20.

———. "What Was Canadian Literature? Taking Stock of the Canlit Industry." *Essays on Canadian Writing* 30 (Winter 1984-85): 17-34.

Mallinson, Jean. *Margaret Atwood and Her Works.* Toronto: ECW, 1984.

Mandel, Eli. *Another Time.* Erin: Press Porcepic, 1977.

———. Ed. *Contexts of Canadian Criticism: A Collection of Critical Essays.* Toronto and Buffalo: University of Toronto Press, 1977.

Markandeya, Kamala. *Nectar in a Sieve.* 1955; rpt. New Delhi: Jaico, 1956.

Maslow, A. H. *The Farther Reaches of Human Nature.* Harmondsworth, Middlesex: Penguin, 1971.

———. *Motivation and Personality.* New York: Harper Row, 1956.

———. *Toward a Psychology of Being.* 2nd ed. New York: D. Van Nostrand, 1968.

Mathews, Robin. "Struggle and Survival in Canadian Literature." *This Magazine is About Schools* 6.4 (Winter 1972-73): 109-24.

May, Rollo. *Love and Will.* New York: Norton, 1969.

———. *Psychological and the Human Dilemma.* Princeton: D. Van Nostrand, 1967. 220.

McCombs, Judith and Carole L. Palmer. *Margaret Atwood: A Reference Guide.* Boston: Hall, 1991.

McCombs, Judith. Ed. *Critical Essays on Margaret Atwood.* Boston: Hall, 1988.

McGee, Mark G. Ed. *Introductory Psychology Reader.* New York: West Publishing Company, 1980.

McGee, Thomas D'Arcy. "Protection for Canadian Literature." *The New Era* (24 April 1958): Rpt. in Ballstadt, 21-24.

———. "The Mental Outfit of the New Dominion." *Speech given in 1867. A Collection of Speeches and Addresses.* Ed. Charles Murphy. Toronto: n.p., 1937. Rpt. in Ballstadt, 91-98.

McMullen, Lorraine. Ed. *Rediscovering Our Foremothers.* Ottawa: University of Ottawa Press, 1990.

Mcpherson, Hugo. "Fiction: 1940-1960." Klinck 2: 205-33.

Mead, George Herbert. *On Social Psychology.* Ed. Anselm Strauss. 1956; rpt. Chicago: University of Chicago Press, 1964.

Mehta, Rohit. *J. Krishnamurti And The Nameless Experience.* Delhi: Motilal Banarsidas, 1973.

Mendez-Egle, Beed. *Margaret Atwood: Reflection and Reality.* Edinburg: Pan American University Press, 1987.

Morton, W. L. *The Canadian Identity.* 1961. 2nd ed. Toronto: University of Toronto press, 1972.

Moss, John. "The English Voice: Invisible Nation." *Modern Fiction Studies* 22.3 (Autumn 1976): 341-45.

———. Ed. "Bushed in the Scared Wood." *The Human Elements* 2nd ser. Ed. Havid Helwing. Ottawa: Oberon Press, 1981. 161-176.

———. *Sex and Violence in the Canadian Novel: The Ancestral Present.* Toronto: McClelland and Stewart, 1977.

———. *The Canadian Novel: Here and Now.* Toronto: NC Press, 1983.

Mowat, Gordon J. "The Purpose of a National Magazine." *Canadian Magazine* XVII (June 1901): 166-67. Rpt. in Ballstadt, 76-79.

Murdoch, Iris. *The Bell*. London: Chatto and Windus, 1958.

Mycak, Sonia. *In Search of the Split Subject: Psychoanalysis, Phenomenology, and the Novels of Margaret Atwood*. Toronto: ECW, 1996.

Narayan, R. K. *The Dark Room*. 1938; rpt. N.D.: Orient Paperbacks, 1978.

Oates, Joyce Carol. *Them*. New York: The Vanguard Press, 1969.

Orwell, Sonia and Angus Ian. Eds. *The Collected Essays: Journalism and Letters of George Orwell, Secker and Warbirg*. 1970, 4 vols. II, p. 134.

Page, James D. *Abnormal Psychology*. 1947; rpt. New Delhi: Tata and McGraw-Hill, 1970.

Paris, Bernard J. *Character and Conflict in Jane Austen's Novels: A Psychological Approach*. Detroit: Wayne State University Press, 1978; Brighton: Harvester Press, 1979.

——. "Third Force Psychology and the Study of Literature." *In Psychological Perspectives on Literature: Freudian Dissidents and Non-Freudians, A Casebook*. Ed. Joseph Natoli. Hamden, CT: Archon, 1984, pp. 155-80.

——. *A Psychological Approach to Fiction: Studies in Thackeray, Stendhal, George Elliot, Dostoevsky, and Conrad*. Bloomington: Indiana University Press, 1974.

——. *Karen Horney: A Psycho-analyst's Search for Self-Understanding*. New Haven and London: Yale University Press, 1994, p. 115.

——. "Experiences of Thomas Hardy." In *The Victorian Experience: The Novelists*. Ed. Richard A. Levine. Athens: Ohio University Press, 1976, pp. 203-37.

——. "Horney's Theory and the Study of Literature." *American Journal of Psychoanalysis* 38 (1978): 343-353.

Powe, B. W. *A Climate Changed: Essays on Canadian Writers*. Oakville, Ont: Mosaic Press, 1984.

Pratt, Annis. *Architypal Patterns in W's Fiction*. Great Britain: The Harvester Press, 1982.

Radway, Janice. *Reading the Romance: Women, Patriarchy and Popular Literature*. North Carolina: University of North Carolina Press, 1984.

Rao, Eleonora. *Strategies for Identity: The Fiction of Margaret Atwood*. New York: Peter Land Publishing, 1994.

Rendon, Mario. "Horney Theory and Literature: A symposium: Introduction." *American Journal of Psychoanalysis* 42 (1982): 3-5.

Rigney, Barbara Hill. *Madness and Sexual Politics in the Feminist Novel: Studies in Brontë, Woolf, Lessing and Atwood.* Wisconsin: University of Wisconsin Press, 1978.

Rosenberg, Jerome H. *Margaret Atwood.* Boston: Twayne Publishers, 1984.

Rusch, Frederik L. "Approaching Literature Through the Social Psychology of Erich Fromm." *In Psychological Perspectives on Literature: Freudian Dissidents and Non-Freudians, A Casebook.* Ed. Joseph Natoli. Hamden, CT: Archon, 1984, pp. 79-99.

Salat, M.F. *Perspectives on Canadian Fiction.* Ed. Sudhakar Pandey. New Delhi: Prestige Books, 1994.

Sandler, Linda. "Interview with Margaret Atwood." *The Malahat Review* 41 (January 1977): 7-27.

———. *Margaret Atwood: Conversations.* Ed. Earl G. Ingersoll. Ontario: Ontario Review Press, 1990.

Sartre, Jean-Paul. *No Exit and Three Other Plays.* New York: Knopf, 1949.

Scheier, Libby., et al. *Language in Her Eye: Views on Writing and Gender by Canadian Women Writing in English.* Toronto: Coach House Press, 1990.

Shahani, Roshan G. "Women as Villains or Victims? The Portrayal of Women in Margaret Atwood's *'The Handmaid's Tale'.*" *The Tropical Maple Leaf: Indian Perspectives in Canadian Studies.* Eds. John L. Hill and Uttam Bhoite. New Delhi: Manohar Publication, 1989.

Sharpe, Martha. "Margaret Atwood and Julia Kristeva: Space-Time, The Dissident Woman Artist, and the Pursuit of Female Solidarity in *'Cat's Eye'.*" *Essays on Canadian Writing*, no. 50 (Fall 1993).

Singh, Sunaina. "Escape as Evolution in *'Lady Oracle'* and *'Where Shall We Go This Summer?'*" *Ambivalence: Studies in Canadian Literature.* Eds. Om P. Juneja and Chandra Mohan. New Delhi: Allied Publishers, 1990.

Singh, Sushila. "Joyce Carol Oates and Margaret Atwood: Two Faces of the New World Feminism." *Punjab University Research Bulletin* 18, no. 1 (1987): 80-102.

Smith, A. J. M. *On Poetry and Poets: Selected Essays of A. J. M. Smith.* Toronto: McClelland and Stewart, 1977.

Smith, Goldwin. "What is the Matter with Canadian Literature?" *The Week* XI (31 August 1864): 950-51. Rpt. in Ballstadt, 85-88.

Staels, Hilde. *Margaret Atwood's Novels: A Study of Narrative Discourse. Transatlantic Perspective.* Tbingen: Francke, 1995.

Staines, David. Ed. *The Canadian Imagination: Dimensions of a Literary Culture.* Cambridge, Mass and London, England: Harvard University Press, 1977.

Steele, Charles. Ed. *Taking Stock: The Calgary Conference on the Canadian Novel.* Downview: ECW press, 1942.

Stevick, Philip. Ed. *The Theory of the Novel.* New York: The Free Press, 1967.

Storr, Anthony. *Human Aggression.* New York: Atheneum, 1968.

Stouck, David. *Major Canadian Authors.* Lincoln and London: University of Nebraska Press, 1988.

Struthers, J. R. (Tim). "An Interview with Margaret Atwood." *Essays on Canadian Writing* 6 (Spring 1977): 18-27.

Sullivan, Rosemary. "An Interview with Margaret Laurence." *A Place to Stand on.* Ed. Woodcock. 61-79.

Thomas, Clara. "'*Lady Oracle*': The Narrative of a Fool-Heroine." *The Art of Margaret Atwood.* Eds. Arnold E. Davidson and Cathy N. Davidson. Toronto: Anansi, 1981.

Thompson, J. Lee. "Can Canada Survive *Survival*? An Article on Survival: 'A Thematic Guide to Canadian Literature'." *American Review of Canadian Studies* 3.2 (Autumn 1973): 101-107.

Thurman, Judith. "When You Wish Upon a Star." *The New Yorker* (29 May 1989): 108-10.

Tomc, Sandra. "The Missionary Position: Feminism and Nationalism in Margaret Atwood's '*The Handmaid's Tale*'." *Canadian Literature,* no. 138/139 (Fall/Winter 1993).

Toye, William. Ed. *The Oxford Companion to Canadian Literature.* Toronto: Oxford University Press, 1983.

Twigg, Alan. "What to Write: Margaret Atwood." *For Openers: Conversations with 24 Canadian Writers.* Madeira Park: Harbour, 1981. 219-30.

Waddington, Miriam. "Canadian Tradition and Canadian Literature." *Journal of Commonwealth Literature* 8 (December 1969): 125-41.

West, Paul. "Ethos and Epic: Aspects of Contemporary Canadian Poetry." *Canadian Literature* 4 (Spring 1960): 7-17. Rpt. in Mandel, Contexts 206-15.

Wiebe, Rudy. *The Scorched-Wood People*. Toronto: MaClelland and Stewart, 1977.

Williams, Tennessee. *27 Wagons Full of Cotton and Other Pays*. New York: New Directions, 1953.

Wine, Jeri Dawn and Janice Ristock. Eds. *Women and Social Change*. Toronto: James Lorimer and Company Publishers, 1991.

Woodcock, George "Margaret Atwood: Poet as Novelist." *The World of Canadian Writing: Critiques and Recollections*. Vancouver: Douglas and Intyre, Seattle: University of Washington Press, 1980. 149-73.

——. *Introducing Margaret Atwood's 'Surfacing'*. Toronto: ECW Press, 1990.

——. "Possessing the Land: Notes on Canadian Fiction." Staines 69-95.

——. Ed. *A Place to Stand on: Essays by and about Margaret Laurence*. Edmonton: NeWest Press, 1983.

Woolf, Virginia. A Writer's Diary. 1953; rpt. New York: New American Library, 1968.

——. *Modern Fiction*. 1919; rpt. London: Hogarth, 1929.

——. "On Re-reading Novel." *Collected Essays*. Vol. 2. London: Hogarth Press, 1966.

——. *The Waves*. 1931; rpt. London: Hogarth Press, 1963.

Yalom, Marilyn. *Maternity, Morality and the Literature of Madness*. London: The Pennsylvania State University Press, 1985. 76-77.

York, Lorraine M. Ed. *Various Atwoods: Essays on the Later Poems, Short Fiction, and Novels*. House of Anansi Press, 1995.

Index